CELESTINA:
GENRE AND RHETORIC

CHARLES F. FRAKER

CELESTINA:
GENRE AND RHETORIC

TAMESIS BOOKS LIMITED
LONDON

Colección Támesis
SERIE A - MONOGRAFIAS, CXXXVIII

DISTRIBUTORS:

Spain:
    Editorial Castalia,
    Zurbano, 39,
    28010 Madrid

United States and Canada:
    Boydell and Brewer, Inc.,
    P. O. Box 41026,
    Rochester, N. Y. 15604, EE.UU.

Great Britain and rest of the world
    Boydell and Brewer Ltd.,
    P. O. Box 9,
    Woodbridge,
    Suffolk, IP12 3DR,
    England

Depósito legal: M. 8082-1990

Printed in Spain by Talleres Gráficos de SELECCIONES GRÁFICAS
Carretera de Irún, km. 11,500 - 28049 Madrid

for
TAMESIS BOOKS LIMITED
LONDON

CONTENTS

FOREWORD

Portions of the study which follows have appeared in print before. The section of Chapter III entitled «Argumentation» is based on two articles of mine, «Rhetoric in the Celestina: *Another Look», in* Aureum Saeculum Hispanum: Beiträge zu Texten des Siglo de Oro, Festschrift für Hans Flasche zum 70. Geburtstag, *ed. Karl-Hermann Körner and Dietrich Briesemeister (Wiesbaden: Franz Steiner, 1982), pp. 81-90, and «Argument in the* Celestina *and its Predecessors», in* Homenaje a Stephen Gilman, Revista de Estudios Hispánicos, *9 (1982 [1984]), 81-86. The first of these is reproduced here entire, the second in part. The section in the same chapter entitled «Style» contains the whole of a third article, «Declamation and the* Celestina», Celestinesca, *9, no. 2 (Autumn 1985), 47-64.*

Celestina is a book one reads all one's life. I believe I first came to know it in the early-to-middle fifties, when I was beginning to be seriously interested in Spanish literature. The first person under whom I studied Celestina, *indeed the only one, was Stephen Gilman. That was in Cambridge, Massachusetts, in the summer of 1957, the year of the publication of* The Art of «La Celestina». *The course was in fact the start of my graduate studies. The end of them also was with Gilman, who was the director of my dissertation. The thesis years were memorable ones, thanks to him. His patience with me then, his encouragement, his generosity to me generally are hard to describe, and now that he has left us I should like to bear public witness to my large debt to him.*

Were he still here, he might have felt that his lessons were not wholly wasted on me: it is a tiny detail, but for a fact The Art of «La Celestina» *has influenced the present study in many ways. But* «Celestina»: Genre and Rhetoric *is not a Gilman book. It is far from insignificant that one portion of it he did get to see displeased him: I in fact take issue with my master more than once. For that very reason I think it important to state that this study of mine was not conceived as polemic: during the months that the themes of this book were taking shape I was thinking in solitude, and a special destiny formed them, for better or for worse. At the time I was writing, naturally enough, I was convinced that Gilman would read what I had produced, and much of the argument of my text can be traced to this circumstance. I did not feel I could simply leave him out of account, and therefore I wished to express my differences with him as respectfully as possible, explaining them as fully as I could. I will go further and say that I wanted very much to win him over. Now, sadly, none of this is going to happen: the reading, the reception favorable or not. In any case «Celestina»: Genre and Rhetoric as it stands is argumentative; I hope it is convincing. But it is not an attack on anyone.*

Special thanks are due to Professor Alan Deyermond, exemplary in every way, who was my generous and long-suffering editor.

Another debt: thanks to my wife, Doris Fraker, for hours and hours of typing.

CHARLES F. FRAKER

University of Michigan,
Ann Arbor.

I

INTRODUCTION

The study which follows is not meant to be a reading of *Celestina*. Except incidentally, it is not about what is distinctive or original in the *Tragicomedia*. My essay owes a great deal in conception and detail to María Rosa Lida de Malkiel's epoch-making examination of Rojas' masterpiece,[1] but my intent and design are in fact the exact opposite of hers. Her great theme is the fundamental independence of *Celestina:* by comparing the work with a large, indeed prodigious, number of control texts she calls our attention to significant differences between it and its fellows, differences deep enough, as she thought, to assure us once for all of that independence. My aim, by contrast, is to show the fundamental solidarity between the great drama and other texts. Although the confrontation between solo and chorus I have in mind is not wholly unlike the one Lida de Malkiel proposes, its sense is not the uniqueness of *Celestina,* but its traditionalism, against appearances.

As the reader will presently discover, the solidarity I am in fact concerned with is a limited one, formal and logical, rather than material and thematic. My broad thesis in these investigations is that *Celestina* is a *normal* work;[2] it is normal in that its basic structure, its fundamental mode of writing, is inherited. Deeply inventive and original as it is, it nevertheless exploits paradigms of literature not of its author's making. It does not set out to lay down statutes for a new kind of literary discourse; nor does it *de facto* or accidentally establish such a discourse. It is composed entirely within discourses existing in its author's day. Many, I assume, would wish to tie its greatness and singularity to opposite premises, to the propositions that would make the *Tragicomedia* more absolutely new. But such a move is surely unnecessary. If *Celestina* is normal, so in a profound sense are *Hamlet* and *Lear*. Greatness in literature, prodigious invention, wide scope, truth, if I may speak in those

---

[1] *La originalidad artística de la 'Celestina'* (Buenos Aires: Eudeba, 1962).

[2] Cfr. the term «normal science» used by THOMAS KUHN in *The Structure of Scientific Revolutions* (Chicago: Chicago Univ. Press, 1970). In using the word «normal» I do not mean to force the analogy between my argument and Kuhn's.

11

terms, are not inevitably bound to structural or paradigmatic novelty. Depth and normality are compatible.

These reflections may prove to be too weighty and pretentious compared with the prosaic investigations that follow. In them I shall be concerned with matters which are local and particular. But limited in scope as they may be, they do claim for themselves a certain significance. One could put it broadly that in some way they set out to do for Rojas and his predecessors what a generation of critics and literary historians in the 1930s and 40s did for Shakespeare, generally to make it possible for readers to understand their author in the light of the high culture of his time, common notions, characterology, moral and political philosophy, rhetoric and literary norms.[3] The scope of my own essay is narrower by far than the one conceived by these scholars, but it is meant to be one in kind with theirs. As concerns *Celestina* studies particularly I cannot at all claim to be the first to work in this mode. In totally different ways Bataillon, and Spitzer in five or six memorable pages, have set out to assimilate the *Tragicomedia* to the ways of thinking and writing of its own age.[4] In principle one would suppose that this was a wholly unremarkable thing to do, to restore a text to its context. But there is also an imbalance to be righted. The present project and others like it go in the face of a powerful current in literary studies. There is a tendency on the part of historians of Spanish literature to value and prize its great masterpieces only in so far as they express a critical attitude towards life and culture. *Celestina,* the *Libro de buen amor,* and *Don Quixote,* so we are told, are all that they are, each uniquely valuable, precisely because they subvert the tradition and put its anomalies on display.[5] Essentially, then, these works are seen as in no way assimilable to the texts preceding and surrounding them; it is this very inheritance they are rebelling against, or in some way holding up to judgment. The premise is, of course, that criticism is a privileged form of discourse, that the man of letters who transcends his own world, stands outside of it, and observes and judges it from his unique position, or more modestly, the one who in his text lays bare the contradictions in that world, is the only one worth taking note of. This is a vulnerable position on several counts. In the

[3] HENRI FLUCHÈRE's *Shakespeare and the Elizabethans* (New York: Hill and Wang, 1956), quite aside from its points of originality, reflects and sums up much of the thought of this generation of commentators.
[4] MARCEL BATAILLON, *La 'Célestine' selon Fernando de Rojas* (Paris: Didier, 1961), and «Gaspar von Barth, interprète de *la Célestine*», *Revue de Littérature Comparée*, 31 (1957), 321-40; LEO SPITZER, «A New Book on the Art of the *Celestina*», *Hispanic Review*, 25 (1957), 1-25. The «five or six memorable pages» I speak of are buried in matter of contrasting character.
[5] An old, influential, and, incidentally, very great example of this mode of commentary is, of course, AMÉRICO CASTRO's classic *El pensamiento de Cervantes, Revista de Filología Española*, anejo 6 (Madrid: Centro de Estudios Históricos, 1925).

first place, the arguments in favor of privileging critical discourse tend, as I believe, to be circular: criticism in a sense affirms its own superiority. Then too, there are many discourses and cultural forms that are quite as powerful as criticism: rhetoric, to my mind, might be an impressive candidate. Finally, criticism in our sense is time-bound and culture-bound: it is the product of a scant two and a half centuries. It is in principle hard to believe that there were no valuable and constructive cultural practices before criticism was invented. Normality, let us insist, is not reductive. A normal text is not critical in an absolute sense, and it does not need to be. It may be combative, argumentative, rhetorical, partisan, but if the forms of discourse of its own time are powerful enough, as they surely were in the days of Rojas and of Cervantes, that text, however ambitious, need not go outside those forms, much less subvert them.

Shakespeare and the Elizabethans is the name of Fluchère's great study. I could attempt a parallel title for my own essay, «Rojas, the First Author and...»; I am not yet ready to complete the syntagma. Both titles are meant to place the authors in question within some sort of tradition. Does Fluchère's title in any way threaten Shakespeare's reputation, or show any lack of admiration for his genius? The question hardly arises. I am, however, haunted by the fear that my own title and the investigations that would follow it might be read as a piece of reductionism, as though putting our play on a level with other texts, tracing its genealogy, or more fundamentally, affirming its normality were simply ways of diminishing the significance of Rojas' masterpiece. As a pledge of good faith I would repeat that the project I am trying to carry out is not meant to be practical criticism. I am making no pretense of capturing or conveying what is memorable or singular in *Celestina*. Let us say the obvious. All the literary norms in the world, all the common notions, all the rhetoric of Quintilian will not write one line of Shakespeare or Rojas, even of a mediocre sonnet or of a boring play. «En esto veo, Melibea, la grandeza de Dios» may have the whole of history behind it, but somebody had to select the matter, frame the sentence, and set it to paper. These very remarks, however, are certainly not meant to be an invitation to stand wordless in admiration before a venerable monument of literature. Least of all are my own studies, which are assuredly not practical criticism, meant to be the last word, foreclosing all possibility of exegesis and interpretation. Practical criticism is still the most difficult of all, and time and circumstance do not make it easier, but it would be foolish to affirm that one could not now or ever say anything intelligent about the uniqueness of *Celestina*. It is also capitally important to insist that positive studies in literature, however austere, are at some point bound to affect the way the texts they deal with are read. The author of these

13

lines, needless to say, is far from indifferent about questions of interpretation in *Celestina*. Again as a pledge of good faith, as evidence that I do take that great work seriously, I shall do now what I do not intend to do henceforth, talk about the excellence of Spain's greatest drama. To bypass dozens of historical problems, and a whole tangle of theoretical difficulties, let me ask one broad unprofessional question. Why has *Celestina* across the years and centuries been so admired and cherished? What has made it in the minds of so many the great treasure of Spanish letters, second only to *Don Quixote*? I believe there are two reasons. One is the complexity and subtlety with which the motives behind the characters' actions are defined and specified. This is not a global matter. Line by line as the dialog unfolds the text makes us understand why Sempronio acts so, why Pármeno says what he does. One can say without sentimentality that time does not diminish this richness: the norms of verisimilitude are not so alien to us nor so bound to a moment in history that we cannot grasp immediately much of what is going on in the play. I shall have a great deal to say about motivation in the body of my study. The second factor is idiom. Not the idiom of the play as a whole: it does not have one. Certainly not the idiom of the author or authors. It is not even reasonable to speak of the idiom of each character: Calisto, Sempronio, Pármeno and the rest will in time speak each in many registers. The idiom of *Celestina* is the idiom of the individual speech, uttered as it is in a particular circumstance of the play's fiction. We should be quite clear as to what we mean by the term. Idiom is not obviously the same as style. In one sense at least, styles in *Celestina* are shared. The sententious Celestina may have a different agenda from the sententious Pármeno. Their personal styles may be miles apart, but their literary styles are virtually the same. Bombast, the mountainous heaps of non-progressive syntagmas, in the mouth of Sempronio is not very different from bombast in Celestina or in Calisto, even though the sense and the tune of their speeches are quite unlike. Idiom is a mix, or conceivably, a multi-deck sandwich. I borrow here in a diffuse way from the rhetorical system of Hermogenes, and from his theory of the Idea: Idea in this concept is very close to what I call idiom.[6] What gives the individual speech its personality is first of all its manifest subject matter: Celestina's speech on old age or Sempronio's on honor, touch on certain themes connected logically in a certain way. Second, there is the speech's

---

[6] HERMOGENES, *De ideis*, in *Opera*, ed. Hugo Rabe (Leipzig: Teubner, 1913), pp. 213-413. Parts of this work are translated by D. A. RUSSELL in *Ancient Literary Criticism*, ed. D. A. Russell and M. Winterbottom (Oxford: Clarendon Press, 1972), pp. 561-79. A good presentation of Hermogenes' system can be found in GERTRUD LINDBERG, *Studies in Hermogenes and Eastathios* (Lund: J. Lindell, 1977). I am using some of Hermogenes' themes for my own purposes, and am not pretending to set forth his system with any accuracy.

micro-disposition, the relative emphasis and space given to one theme in contrast to another, the flow of discourse, the way one topic gives way to the next, the whole layout of the piece. The third element is style, properly speaking, choice of words, register, syntax, rhythm, figures of speech. A study of the particular profile and personality of a passage from *Celestina,* what I call the idiom of the speech, might have to take all of these factors into account. The richness and variety, the subtlety and exactness of idiom in any particular case, and all that this total manner conveys, all this is surely one of the things that sets *Celestina* apart. What, for example, gives such character and drama to the old woman's speech in the twelfth act, in which she refuses to give up the gold chain?[7] I shall not claim to do a full Hermogenean analysis. It is a total speech, and every part of it works, but it would seem to be its logical structure, its plain anomalies that are most expressive, this along with its micro-disposition, moving informally from one subject to the next. Have you taken leave of your senses, says Celestina; am I obliged to pay your expenses and not Calisto? My share-and-share-alike speech addressed to you was not in earnest. The chain has gone astray. I gave it to Elicia to play with and it was lost, perhaps stolen, a pity, not because it was valuable, but because one hates bad luck. I earned fully everything Calisto gave me. I in turn don't lay claim to anything he gave you. These gifts are my livelihood; any extra items you acquire are luxury. If the chain does turn up, we'll do what we can; in the meantime you have my good will. Thus far the simple content of the speech. One notes the plain incompatibility of its two lines of argument, on one hand «Calisto's gifts to me are mine alone, by right», and on the other, «the chain is lost, but was not of much value anyway». And yet pragmatically the two strains are not contradictory. The clash of themes simply tells Sempronio and the reader that the story about the chain is a transparent lie meant to convince no one. Hence the *ethos* of the speech, which not only states Celestina's right as she sees it, but her contempt for the young men and her total self-assurance in stating her claim. Celestina emphasizes, and she also diminishes. She diminishes her promise to share, the basis for her servant's claim: «te as asido a una *palabrilla*», says she. She diminishes the value of the chain, a plaything for Elicia easily lost, of no great worth in any case. The chain is, of course, very precious, and so her lie is a broadly imperious dismissal of the youth's claim. Idiom is, then, *ethos* reduced to the information, the logic and the linguistic and discursive devices of the speech. Virtually all but the briefest

---

[7] FERNANDO DE ROJAS, *Celestina: Tragicomedia de Calisto y Melibea,* ed. Miguel Marciales, Illinois Medieval Monographs, 1 (Urbana: Univ. of Illinois Press, 1985), vol. II, *Edición crítica,* Act 12, *versículos* 79-87. Quotations and references will be to this edition, identifying passages as Marciales suggests, by act and *versículo,* e.g. «XII. 79-87».

and most peripheral speeches in *Celestina* have each their own ethos and idiom, and rarely is this ethos sustained in a way less complicated than in Celestina's chain piece. It is in great part this astonishing richness and complexity of meaning in *Celestina,* part by part and as a whole, that catapults it to greatness, that makes it not only literally different from more or less comparable texts, but puts it on a higher plane, as one of the most remarkable works in its language and of its time, indeed of many times.

I have not tried to analyze the chain speech to display my talents as a critic, which are in any case modest. I can justify this discussion of the practical criticism of *Celestina* in two ways, by showing what form I think that criticism should take, and by making it clear that the reflections which follow, which may at times take on the look of «close reading», are not that criticism, and are not meant to be. It is easy to be misread. Poetics in certain of its forms takes on the look of exegesis, especially when it makes us fix our gaze on the details of one text or a small body of texts. In this case, so it would seem, the commentator is surely trying to lay bare the heart of these utterances, their inner substance. All of this would amount to a simple misunderstanding: he is doing nothing of the kind. There are, however, two points worth making. The first is that literary studies which are not primarily interpretative cannot fail at some point to influence the way the texts under study are read. The second is that investigations like the ones which follow, concerned as they are with genre, with literary norms, with rhetoric, should actually prepare the way for such a finer understanding. The reason for this is obvious. Studies like mine set out to make explicit the very rules that can render an intelligent reading possible. If interpretation is the final stage of a total commentary, essays in the style of this one could represent the penultimate step, the final clearing of the decks. The lines that follow are not exegesis, but I hope that some will find *Celestina* more transparent, more intelligible, even more moving on their account.

II

GENRE

«Speak of the devil», says Areúsa in effect as Sosia is at her door: «el lobo es en la conseja» (XVII. 12). This striking expression is proverbial, and is recorded by Correas.[1] It must also have been proverbial in Terence's time. In the *Adelphoe* Ctesipho and Syrus are speaking of the young man's father; Demea at that very moment appears, and the slave says, «the wolf in the fable».[2] The coincidence is surely notable. In *Celestina* once again, when we first see Areúsa speaking with Centurio at the beginning of Act XV, she is heaping him with reproaches: after all her gifts to him, after all she has done, he will not grant her one small favor. In Act XVIII we discover what her request was: «le rogué estotro día que fuesse una jornada de aquí, en que me iva la vida» (XVIIIa. 4). Areúsa's motive is not specified, but the situation is plainly a copy of the one between Phaedria and the courtesan in the *Eunuchus*: Thais must wheedle the slave-girl away from Thraso, and so implores her lover to leave Athens for a while so she can give all her attention to the soldier.

There are Terentian reminiscences in the post-1499 section of the text that turn on weightier matters, as we shall see. The added acts are, superficially at least, a mixed blessing. Certain strains in them are surely part of the fundmental *Celestina*, our *Celestina*; it is difficult to imagine the drama without them. Other parts go down less easily.[3] Thus on one

---

[1] GONZALO CORREAS, *Vocabulario de refranes y frases proverbiales*, ed. Louis Combet (Bordeaux: Institut d'Etudes Ibériques et Ibéro-Américaines, 1967), no. 81: «El lobo en la conseja», quoted in *La Celestina*, ed. Julio Cejador y Frauca, Clásicos Castellanos, 20 & 23 (Madrid: La Lectura, 1913; rpt. Espasa-Calpe, 1958), II, p. 157, n. 1.

[2] *P. Terenti Afri Comoediae*, ed. Robert Kauer and Wallace M. Lindsay (Oxford: Clarendon, 1958), *Adelphoe*, line 537. References to Terence will henceforth be by line-number from this edition. Translations of Terence are from *The Comedies*, trans. Betty Radice (Harmondsworth: Penguin Books, 1965); since this translation indicates the lines in the original, it will be unnecessary to cite the pages.

[3] MARCIALES regards the *Tratado de Centurio*, as he defines it, as a graft onto *Celestina*, and not by Rojas. The *Tratado* consists of those scenes that bear on the intrigue Areúsa-Elicia-Centurio. In my opinion, Marciales, brilliant and learned, floats hypotheses about *Celestina* which are very unequal in value. For reasons too complicated to discuss here I shall continue treating this group of passages

17

hand there is Calisto's long soliloquy after the first night of love, one of the great moments in the play, thematically important, and one which brings depth and perspective to our picture of this, the central character. Then too, there are the scenes in which we see the new Melibea, transformed by her love experience. Finally, we are given Pleberio, in a full-length portrait. Without the additional acts we should have only the final speech along with a few scraps of one other scene, hardly enough to give us much of an understanding of the knowing and secure father of the heroine. The embarrassment comes from the other strain, the intrigue involving Elicia, Areúsa and Centurio. This line of plot strikes one as curiously inorganic, absolutely and in comparison to the elements I have mentioned. It is ill-motivated, and seems to lead nowhere. Areúsa, not notable for her singlemindedness in love, hatches the scheme of taking revenge for the deaths of Pármeno and Sempronio. This is hardly verisimilar: her liaison with Calisto's young servant cannot have lasted very long, although one must confess that the chronology of the work is never very clear. In any case, she accepts him as a lover, not out of native inclination, but under strong pressure from Celestina. What is worse, she abandons him, even before she knows he is dead, for a man she is obsessed with, a man she has showered with gifts and whose welfare she has looked after. It is, of course, entirely wrong to expect an author of the Renaissance to spin out a web of motivation as a classic novelist might, but the least we can say is that Areúsa's reasons for wanting Calisto dead are not fully explained. It could be argued on the basis of the dinner at Celestina's house that both prostitutes harbor bitterness of long standing against Melibea, but even here the basis for this hatred is not made very clear to us: it is certainly not anchored in the particulars of the lives of the three women, Elicia, Areúsa and Melibea. Motivation aside, the whole plot seems to run into a dead end: Centurio, who is to do the dirty work, is a coward, and hands the bloody task over to Traso. Traso and his men are hardly more valorous: they only feign an attack, Tristán and Sosia have no difficulty putting them to flight, and so in the short run the plan is foiled. But then, strangest of all, Areúsa's ends are realized by the purest accident, no thanks to her or her supposed allies. Calisto leaves Melibea's garden in haste, misses his footing on the ladder, falls to the street and is killed. This whole disposition of the plot of *Celestina* is strange, especially if we think how solidly the play is motivated otherwise. Now, in fairness, if one were to ask if the episode added anything to the sixteen-act *Comedia,* one would of course have to answer affirmatively. It makes Calisto's death more plausible. In the 1499 *Celestina* the young man's bad luck is spectacular: he has just made love to Me-

as a wholly legitimate part of the *Tragicomedia*. For one version of Marciales' argument see his vol. II, p. 273, first note.

libea for the first time when fate swings her axe for no reason at all: the misstep is pure accident. But in the new version, not so: Calisto hears Sosia's voice, thinks his servant is in some danger, sets out in great haste to help him, and does not even bother to put on his armor; he rushes to the top of the wall, falls and dies. We must remember that in the new version this is not the first time that Calisto has clambered in and out of the garden in the dark. That he should miss his footing on the thirtieth try is more plausible than that he should on the first, especially if on the thirtieth he left in haste.

But for all of this Rojas takes us the long way around the barn. Do we really need Areúsa's plan of revenge, her previous connection with Centurio, her elaborate trick to get Sosia to tell her when Calisto would be abroad, her second dialogue with Centurio, and then Centurio's passing the charge on to Traso, all and exclusively to explain why Calisto fell from the ladder? The whole stretch of plot is odd. But perhaps there is less randomness here than appears at first glance. One feature of this minidrama is a contrast: a plain confrontation between two forces, what certain of the characters set out to do and what Fortune in the end actually brings about. Areúsa along with Elicia plans to have Calisto destroyed: the plan fails, but by the strangest chance Calisto dies anyway. The very wildness of the coincidence is plainly and obviously supposed to embody one of the most basic characteristics of Fortune, her caprice. The more capricious chance is, the more truly is she chance. Now Fortune is one of the leading actors in our great drama: an interpretation of *Celestina* that does not take her into account would have to be an odd one indeed. In the large main plot of the *Tragicomedia* there is, trivially, also a contrast between what the human agents intend and what Fortune finally disposes. Calisto and Melibea, seconded by Sempronio and then Celestina, set out to have a love affair, but the fatal slip on the ladder puts a stop to such plans. The contrast here is less freakish, but by no means less significant. Could it be that the secondary intrigue with Areúsa, Elicia, Centurio and all the rest was meant to dramatize still more the contrast between what humans intend and what actually comes to pass? Is it not possible that the special irony of this sub-drama, the fact that chance really does bring about what the principals intend, brings the whole contrast into still higher relief?

Before we dismiss such a reading of *Celestina* as over-subtle or as notorious overinterpretation, there are certain facts one should bring to mind. There is a literary text very well known to Rojas which not only contains plots very much like that of the Areúsa-Centurio intrigue, but which also highlights the very theme we are concerned with: «man proposes, but God/Fate disposes.» This text is the group of six comedies of Terence, a school text, known to virtually anyone literate in Latin in

19

Rojas' time. In five of the six plays pure chance fulfills the desires of at least one of the principal characters. In two, *Andria* and *Phormio,* we get situations especially like the one in the Areúsa-Centurio episode. In both a beneficent schemer lays hold of every trick he can think of to flatten the obstacles in the lover's path, but in both his brilliance is in vain, since pure circumstance is what works the solution. It is, of course, striking and significant that the good fortune in the plays of Terence has been turned into evil fortune in *Celestina,* but across the board we can affirm that fictional plots of this species were devised to dramatize precisely the theme of the fortuitous. It is by no means pure coincidence that the modern critical tradition has put such stress on the theme of Fortune in the New Comedy and on the philosophical background of that strain.[4] And it is also far from unlikely that a writer of the late fifteenth century, working at a time when the theme of Fortune was sounded loudly in a great many literary texts, should also have taken note of the importance of the theme in the one segment of the New Comedy best known to him. The Areúsa-Centurio intrigue remains something of an anomaly, though perhaps less so once we get close to it. In any case the best explanation for such an oddity in the twenty-one act *Celestina* may be precisely the fact that Rojas was trying to imitate Terence.

Terentian or more generally Roman influence in *Celestina* is a complicated and problematic subject. All attempts to put the tragicomedy into the same bag as Terence and Plautus come up against the plain fact that taken as a whole our drama is not very much like a Roman comedy. But even here there is a factor which, as far as I know, has never been fully considered. I mean the structure and design of the first act. Rojas sewed the seam between this unfinished work and his own with great skill, and it is hard to think of the two bits separately. But if we do keep before our minds the outlines of the primitive *Celestina,* separate from the material Rojas added to it, we are confronted with a fragment that is much more Roman than Rojas' work, more Roman indeed than most examples of the humanistic comedy, the genre we nowadays normally associate with our text. I should call the first act a modern adaptation of a Roman pattern. Its author was not trying to produce a copy that could be mistaken for the original: he was setting out to produce a contemporary analogue. Some of the material was modern, but the mold was ancient. A distraught lover, with his mocking, but ultimately helpful, servant: does the pattern seem alien to the old texts, a betrayal of their spirit and mood? Obviously not. What is more, such a scene actually does occur in a Roman play: the first scene of Plautus' *Pseudolus* has

---

⁴ See, for example, R. L. HUNTER, *The New Comedy of Greece and Rome* (Cambridge: Univ. Press, 1985), pp. 141 ff.

roughly the same pair, a lover obsessed to the point of being ridiculous, and a witty and knowing slave who laughs first, but finally uses his mental resources to try to unite the young man with his love. The first act also has the pair of servants, a wily one who encourages Calisto's love, and another plain-spoken one who advises caution. Twinning in Roman comedy is of course everywhere. Early on in *Andria,* for example, we meet Sosia, trustworthy retainer, freed by his old master, and the artful Davus, entirely at the disposal of the young lover. And in particular the figure of the slave who is prudent and discourages his young master's excesses is far from unknown in the old plays. Pármeno's namesake in the *Eunuchus* tries to keep Chaerea from impersonating the eunuch, and Messenio, the slave in Plautus' play, heaps good counsel on Menaechmus. Even the figure of Celestina, obviously and patently of a type alien to the New Comedy, could pass as an analogue to certain of the most hateful type-characters in Terence and Plautus, the pander, the slave merchant. Then too, there is a prostitute in our famous first act: she is light-years away from the elegant courtesans of the New Comedy, but is legally a prostitute, none the less, and is, once again, a clear analogue. Most important of all, perhaps, is what, thanks to circumstances, is not in the first act, what cannot be read there. What would the complete primitive *Celestina* have been like? How would it have been continued? How would it have ended? Bataillon tried to convince us years ago that our text was a fragment of a comedy, a play with a happy ending, and that Rojas' blood and pathos was a betrayal of its soul and spirit.[5] Is the comic character of the first act, taking «comic» in its most obvious sense, so peripheral or unimportant? Let us suppose that tomorrow an investigator in the Biblioteca Nacional should find a manuscript of the entire non-Rojas *Celestina,* and let us further suppose that we read there that Sempronio, along with the old bawd, wove a complicated web of deceit at the expense of Pleberio and of Calisto's own father (why should he not have one?) so that the young man could have his wish: imagine further that the work ended with some sort of marriage (secret, perhaps) brought about either by good luck, or by the machinations of Celestina and the servant. In other words let us plot out our imaginary *Celestina* more or less on the model of a Roman play. If such a text should actually turn up, should we have any right to be surprised? There is a serious issue here. The primitive *Celestina* might have ended in any one of a dozen different ways, but our fragment has nothing in it that would exclude a development and ending something like that of a genuine ancient comedy. Indeed, in the order of things, that solution would have been much more verisimilar than

---

[5] MARCEL BATAILLON, «La *Célestine primitive*», in *Studia philologica et litteraria in honorem L. Spitzer* (Bern: Francke, 1958), pp. 39-55: the essay also appears as a chapter in *La «Célestine» selon Fernando de Rojas.*

the one history actually produced: no learned hypothesis in the world could possibly have foreseen *Celestina* as Rojas wrote it.

The first author meant to produce a modern analogue. It is almost unnecessary to point out the features of his work which could have no place in an old play. The first scene is obviously and notoriously un-ancient.[6]. The concept of love generally is of the author's day, love as pathology, love as idolatry, and not that of Terence. And as I have mentioned, the Celestina figure, whose history is well-known, does not belong to the New Comedy. Although the author does include a prostitute in his play, she is wholly unlike the analogous figures in ancient comedy. Most important of all, the moral tone of the first act is wholly its own. Calisto's obsession is not the pardonable frailty Terence would have given us, but something darker. Celestina, even in the first act, is a more formidable evil character than the most hateful pander in Plautus. To serve her own interests she is willing to win Pármeno away from everything that serves his. The boy has climbed from a wretched position to a comfortable and secure one, but Celestina has no scruples about trying to return him to his first state. No character in all of the New Comedy is as elaborately evil as this.

* * *

The first act, then, gives us a mixture of old and relatively new. But of the two the one that needs to be stressed is the old, the large framework, the broad outline. Both our authors, therefore, Rojas and his predecessor, attended to Terence and Plautus, and followed them, not only in random details, but in features close to the center of their conceptions. Did this attention extend to still other aspects of the Roman theater which are even more fundamental? Were the Terentian touches in the two parts of *Celestina* something simply local, ornaments in a drama of very different character overall, or are they a sign of a larger intention? Were our two authors actually attempting to write a Roman play, or short of that, a work within the same genre as those of Terence and Plautus? The lines that follow are in effect a piece of exegesis on a remarkable text, consisting of two words «terenciana obra», words written by Fernando de Rojas about the first act.[7] What could its author have meant by this? More pertinently, would Rojas himself ever have thought the expression applicable to his own work? And if so, would such a view have been a bad mistake? If we do believe that *Celestina* is «terenciana», saying so would come close to what ancients called a paradox, the pro-

---

[6] MARCIALES, be it noted, expresses doubts that the first scene is by the first author (whom he believes to be Cota): *Celestina*, I, pp. 70-72.

[7] OA. 9.

position against the grain like «the virtuous poor are happy», or «fools are sometimes wiser than their fellows». The *Tragicomedia* has on the face of it very little in common with the plays of Terence and Plautus: rule out a few obvious parallelisms and we have a drama of very different intention and scope. If in the face of this dissimilarity we wish to call Rojas' work «terenciana», we shall surely be going in the face of common sense: if it is true, it is an unlikely truth. But perhaps the likeness or unlikeness that hits us in the eyes has little to do with the matter. Suppose we raise the issue of genre. Works in the same genre can be very dissimilar. No two pieces of music could be more unlike than any one of the London symphonies of Johann Christian Bach and Mahler's Ninth, but we have no basis at all for denying that they are both symphonies: the formal grounds are there, and no difference in the size of the two works, in their instrumentation, in their affect, or even in a broad sense in their intention can erode this basis. How do we stand on the question of the genre of *Celestina*? The whole problem of *Celestina* as Roman comedy has in fact been aired once before. María Rosa Lida de Malkiel begins her chapter on the genre of the work:

> Si dentro de alguna tradición literaria de la Europa Occidental se quiere encuadrar esta obra, ha de pensarse en primer lugar en la llamada «comedia nueva», esto es, la de Menandro, transmitida a los tiempos medios y modernos por Plauto y Terencio. (*Originalidad*, p. 29)

She quotes immediately the introductory verses of *Celestina* in which Rojas praises the original fragment, which he in his own day describes as «terenciana». Lida de Malkiel paraphrases and explicates Urrea's text: «terenciana obra» means simply «obra dramática», and «terenciana» in particular only identifies Rojas' work as a play about love, like Terence's, further parallels counting for little. «Todo examen de la *Celestina*», she then declares, «confirma esta conclusión» (p. 30). In the lines and pages following she considers three different kinds of «Terentian» texts which might have served as models for *Celestina*, the Roman plays themselves, the twelfth-century elegiac comedies, and the Latin humanistic plays of the fifteenth century. But whereas the first two species contribute to the Spanish play only locally and partially, the humanistic comedy influences it more fundamentally: *Celestina* virtually is a member of this kind, rogue only in that it is written in a vernacular.

This is surely not an unreasonable account of the whole complicated matter. But it is to my mind lacking mainly because it does not make the case for the Roman inheritance strong enough. In considering all these species of drama Lida de Malkiel brings a modern perspective: to our eyes Roman and elegiac plays show only limited parallels to *Celestina*, whereas the humanistic share with it more fundamental traits. Love comedy would be the only Terentian note that would fit all of these texts.

23

That is the way things look to us. But supposing instead we began with a more powerful notion of the comic genre, one accessible to the tragico-medy's two authors, to Jiménez de Urrea and to their contemporaries. Then, perhaps, practical differences between Roman, humanistic and other plays would become less significant, and we could perceive important traits they all shared. «Terenciana obra» applied to *Celestina* should be a pregnant phrase. I shall attempt to show that Rojas and his prede-cessors indeed set out to compose a Terentian work, a Roman comedy in a sense much stronger than Lida de Malkiel allows, and that its genre as they perceived it was «comedy» simply. I shall further argue that the famous humanistic plays do not belong to a separate genre, but that in the minds of all concerned these also were simply comedies, without qualification.

So, as I would have it, all wind up traveling on the same boat, Plautus, Terence, Ugolino da Pisa, the author of the first act, and Fernando de Rojas. How powerful is this notion of genre? Could the list be extended to include Shakespeare, Lope de Vega, Molière or Terence Rattigan (an-other Terence)? Not necessarily and in some cases assuredly not. What is pertinent here is what Rojas might have thought constituted comedy, and not some broader or more inclusive concept. Let us return to a problem I have alluded to, the presumed differences between Rojas's work and its models. One great difficulty is the fact that at first glance all but a few of the Roman comedies seem to have a prodigious likeness to each other. They are riddled with formulae of all sorts. The same characters reappear, the severe father, the indulgent one, the impatient young lover, the *servus callidus,* the elegant prostitute, and so on. The same sort of thing happens in many of the plays. The frustrated lover puts all of his confidence in the wily slave who invents elaborate plots for his young master's sake; the winsome young woman in humiliating circumstances turns out to have been free-born, or related to one of the principals. For us, perhaps, this whole set of clichés is the New Comedy, and it is of course significant that when humanists in the sixteenth century tried to write Terentian plays, they took over as much of this apparatus as they could. But our view of Terence and Plautus and the humanistic comedy is not necessarily the same as Rojas' or that of any of the authors of the great Latin plays of the fifteenth century. Here are two texts which must have been known to Rojas, which are almost certainly about comedy, and which in fact sixteenth-century commentators on Terence applied to comedy. One is from Cicero's *De inventione.* There is a kind of narrative, Cicero says, that focuses not only on events, but on the words and per-sonal attitudes of the characters. In such a narrative we must include «fluctuations of fortune, contrast of characters, severity, gentleness, hope, fear, suspicion, desire, dissimulation, delusion, pity, sudden change of fortune, unexpected disaster, sudden pleasure, a happy ending to the story». Practically the same passage appears in the *Rhetorica ad Herennium*.[8] In these very prestigious texts about comedy which any budding humanist would have been obliged to study there is only one theme which is obviously not applicable to *Celestina*: this is the «happy ending to the story». What to my mind is supremely interesting about this utterance of Cicero is that while it is by any standards an accurate general description of the plays of Terence, Plautus and their Greek forebears, at the same time its statute is broad enough to cover *Celestina*. I shall at this point cite together a Renaissance authority and one of his latter-day commentators, who together make a point which is illuminating. The authority is Scaliger, who is giving us his definition of comedy: «Comoedia igitur sic definiamus nos, poema dramaticum, *negotiosum*, exitu laeto, stylo populari». Katherine Ernestine Wheatley in her study of Terence and Molière introduces the above quotation as follows:

> Neither the practice of Terence nor Donatus' theories would demand that comedy be filled with intrigue. Scaliger is the first theorist to define comedy as a dramatic poem filled with intrigue and full of action [9].

(Donatus is, of course, the greatest ancient commentator on Terence.) The point of these quotations is much the same as the one I drew from Cicero. Conventionally, out of inertia, perhaps, we believe that Roman comedies are full of intrigue, that the intrigue is one of the things that define them. Scaliger thought about the matter just as we do, and yet, as it turns out, he was the first in history to put the intrigue-factor, the *negotiosum*, into the definition. *Celestina* does not fit inside his definition, since its action is fairly simple, since it does not have a complicated plot. But as far as intrigue is concerned, Rojas and the older Donatus can live together in peace: the old commentator would not have exiled Rojas or his *comedia* on that score.

What we need to do is to accumulate texts about comedy which Rojas would have known and thought authoritative which do what Cicero's does, which gives us a fair account of the old plays, but which are not so narrow as to exclude *Celestina* wholly. The statutes such texts lay down must include and exclude: they must be broad enough to include both Plautus and Rojas and yet be narrow enough to define something, to be an effective norm. The task is not difficult on either score, access-

---

[8] *De inventione*, I, 27, translated by H. M. Hubbell in Cicero, *De inventione, De optimo genere oratorum, Topica* (Cambridge, MA: Harvard Univ. Press; London: William Heinemann, 1949); *Ad Herennium*, ed. and trans. Harry Caplan (same publishers, 1954), I.13. For the influence of the latter passage during the Renaissance see EDWIN W. ROBBINS, *Dramatic Characterization in Printed Commentaries on Terence 1473-1600* (Urbana: Univ. of Illinois Press, 1951), p. 40.

[9] *Molière and Terence: A Study in Molière's Realism* (Austin: Univ. of Texas Press, 1931), p. 109. The italics in the quotation from Scaliger are Wheatley's.

ibility and authority on one hand, or definitiveness on the other. Ancient definitions of comedy that Rojas might have known are remarkably uniform, and the Renaissance texts, which at the very least tell us what current school teaching was like, are quite faithful to the old authorities (see Robbins, pp.15-37). The burden of all these utterances is that comedy is a representation of the doings and the fortunes of people of ordinary or middle status, in the course of which fictional action there is no danger to life. A corollary to this general proposition is that the comedy is broadly speaking realistic, that it is faithful in detail to life. There is the tidy account of the grammarian Diomedes, a text that in one form or another circulated widely and which Rojas may have seen: comedy is an «expression of private and civil fortune without peril to life». Diomedes contrasts comedy and tragedy:

> Comedy differs from tragedy in the fact that in tragedy great men, leaders, and kings are introduced, while in comedy humble and private individuals are represented; that in the former are lamentations, exiles, and murders, and in the latter amours and rapes of sorrowful maidens; and accordingly, in the fact that in the former there are frequently and almost always successful conclusions to joyful affairs and the recognition, for the worse, of children and former events. (Quoted in Robbins, p. 7)

One might observe in passing that our little bugbear, the happy ending, is in Diomedes hedged in by an «almost always». Copies of the all-important Terence commentary of the grammarian Aelius Donatus were normally prefaced by two short treatises on comedy, Evanthius' *De fabula,* and *De comoedia* of Donatus himself (in older editions presented as a single piece all attributed to Donatus). Evanthius has the following:

> hoc igitur quod supra diximus malo coacti omittere satyram aliud genus carminis νέαν κωμῳδίαν, hoc est nouam comoediam, repperere poetae, quae argumento communi magis et generaliter ad omnes homines, qui mediocribus fortunis agunt, pertineret et minus amaritudinis spectatoribus et eadem opera multum delectationis afferret, concinna argumento, consuetudini congrua, utilis sententiis, grata salibus, apta metro [10].

Meter aside, the one stumbling block here is, of course, the «minus amaritudinis spectatoribus», the supposed light tone of comedy. But even here there is a qualifying clause. Evanthius, comparing Terence to other composers of comedy, writes of the former:

> illud est admirandum, quod et morem retinuit, ut comoediam scriberet, et temperauit affectum, ne in tragoediam transiliret. quod cum aliis rebus

---

[10] *Aeli Donati commentum Terenti,* ed. Paulus Wessner (Leipzig: Teubner, 1902-03), I, II.6. In Wessner the chapters in Evanthius' treatise and Donatus' are numbered as though they were a single work. References henceforth to Evanthius and to Donatus' *De comoedia* will be to this edition.

minime obtentum et a Plauto et ab Afranio, et appio et multis fere magnis comicis inuenimus. illud quoque inter Terentianas uirtutes mirabile, quod eius fabulae eo sunt temperamento, ut neque extumescant ad tragicam celsitudinem neque abiciantur ad mimicam uilitatem. (III 5)

Terence, says Evanthius, is unique among comic poets in that his plays do not veer off either into tragedy or farce: Plautus and others are not so scrupulous. Rojas, author of a tragicomedy, might well have taken note that by Evanthius' word some poets did so swerve. Our critic's fullest statement comes in his comparison of comedy and tragedy:

inter tragoediam autem et comoediam cum multa tum inprimis hoc distat, quod in comoedia mediocres fortunae hominum, parui impetus periculorum laetique sunt exitus actionum, at in tragoedia omnia contra, ingentes personae, magni timores, exitus funesti habentur; et illic prima turbulenta, tranquilla ultima, in tragoedia contrario ordine res aguntur; tum quod in tragoedia fugienda uita, in comoedia capessenda exprimitur; postremo quod omnis comoedia de fictis est argumentis, tragoedia saepe de historia fide petitur. (IV 2)

Once again, our difficulty is the happy outcome. We shall hear more from Evanthius further along.

Donatus' essay on comedy offers us God's plenty at the start:

Comoedia est fabula diuersa instituta continens affectuum ciuilium ac priuatorum, quibus discitur, quid sit in uita utile, quid contra euitandum... comoediam esse Cicero ait imitationem uitae, speculum consuetudinis, imaginem ueritatis. comoediae autem more antiquo dictae, quia in uicis huiusmodi carmina initio agebantur apud Graecos... quo, dum actus commutantur, populus attinebatur απὸ τῆς κώμης, hoc est ab actu uitae hominum, qui in uicis habitant ob mediocritatem fortunarum, non in aulis regiis, ut sunt personae tragicae. comoedia autem, quia poema sub imitatione uitae atque morum similitudine compositum est, in gestu et pronuntiatione consistit. comoediam apud Graecos dubium est quis primus inuenerit, apud Romanos certum: et comoediam et tragoediam et togatam primus Liuius Andronicus repperit. aitque esse comoediam cotidianae uitae speculum, nec iniuria. nam ut intenti speculo ueritatis liniamenta facile per imaginem colligimus, ita lectione comoediae imitationem uitae consuetudinisque non aegerrime animaduertimus. (V 1-5)

We must observe that among all these utterances only the quotation from Livius Andronicus tells us that comedy must avoid the dark side. And although in fact no surviving comedy of the two Romans or their predecessors has an unhappy ending, that particular constraint, the happy outcome, is not much emphasized in this set of propositions. Rojas, if he knew this passage from Donatus, would not therefore have thought his breaches of the comic code, the pathos and deaths, a very serious violation.

Comedy, then, must be about the ordinary deeds of people of moderate fortune, and it must be realistic. Those are the two remaining themes

(along with the happy ending and the bright tone) stated in our authorities. For the critic this sets one easy target and a nearly impossible one.
It hardly demands great intellect to determine whether a play is or is not
about people of middle station, but how once for all are we going to
decide responsibly and with rigor if it is realistic? How can we frame a
plausible and reasonable standard for verisimilitude? Once again, Donatus
may be the one to turn to, author of an extensive and many-faceted text
on Terence and on comedy which was for long years normative. The
large collection of scholia on Terence with its introductory matter, all
attributed to Aelius Donatus, is, of course, one of the most frequently
copied and printed texts in Europe over centuries.[11] Terence was, after
all, a school text, one demanding explication, and the great popularity
of Donatus the expositor has to do with this fact. His text at the very
least tells us what a latter-day grammarian's commentary might be like;
Rojas, if he did not know Donatus' great work directly, would surely
have known a good deal of its substance. Now what does this large
collection contribute generally to our understanding of comedy as a genre,
and more particularly to the notion of realism in comedy, or, indeed, of
realism in general? My answer may come as an anticlimax. The commentary attributed to Donatus assigns motives to the actions and speeches
of Terence's characters, and it does so frequently. Why at the beginning
of *Andria* does Simo order the slaves to carry all the supplies into the
house? Donatus tells us: it is so that he can speak alone and in confidence to his freedman Sosia. Simple comments like this are legion; they
decorate nearly every page of the commentary from one end to another.
As I say, this may seem like an unspectacular trait, however prominent.
For one thing Donatus is not alone. Many ancient commentaries on the
poets point out and specify motives just as his does. Why was Iarbas
angry at his father Jupiter? Servius in his commentary on the *Aeneid*
tells us. Why did Ascanius shoot the fawn? Servius, once again, tells us.
One ancient commentary, that of Tiberius Donatus, also on the *Aeneid,*
is made up entirely of two strains, the pointing out of rhetorical devices
in the poem and the specifying of motives, quite in the style of Donatus
and Servius. There are, however, two reasons why this characteristic is
significant, why taking note of it is far from trivial. First, in any older
commentary on a prestigious ancient poet verisimilitude is bound to be
an issue. This judgment should astonish no one. Faithfulness to life has
been a major theme in poetics from Aristotle's time to our own, and in
fact expositors have over the centuries vindicated the verisimilitude of

---

[11] See, for example, MAX MANITIUS, *Handschriften antiker Autoren in mittelalterlichen Bibliotekskatalogen* (Leipzig: Otto Harrassowitz, 1935), pp. 12-16. Another good testimony is the *Praefatio* in H. T. Karsten's edition of *Commenti Donatiani* (Leiden: A. W. Sijthoff, 1912), I, pp. i-xxi.

their texts one step at a time, pointing out the plausibility of first one detail of the story and then another. We shall return to this matter in time. The second reason why Donatus' signalling of motives might be pertinent to a study of Rojas is that the very frequency of these markings is a distinctive feature, one which seriously reflects the substance and significance of the text. We must begin by pointing out that the high count of motive-comments in Donatus does indeed correspond to something in the plays themselves. For him to treat them as he does they must be susceptible to such treatment. That is to say, if Donatus is going to point out motives in the plays several times on a page, the plots themselves must have many turns that depend on the characters' intentions and which are therefore explainable as based on our general understanding of human motives. But if we join this characteristic with the constraint that comedy be about the ordinary doings of people of moderate fortune, the list of possible motivations we can expect to find in a play is reduced. For example, the things that might motivate a statesman or a warrior are obviously ruled out. But there is a further issue. In what kind of narrative should we expect to find a great frequency of motivated actions and speeches? How often do we have to know why Aeneas acts as he does, or Turnus? Heroic and tragic texts are spacious and monumental, and a very few critical moments per episode are quite enough. There are, for a fact, well-known tragedies in which no more than three or four things happen, in which the motivated turns of plot I have spoken of can be counted on the fingers of one hand. But if we reduce our scale, forget about heroic acts loaded with public significance and focus instead on the ordinary deeds of ordinary men and women, then every detail becomes interesting, and we may expect small crises to occur very frequently. To my mind, this very combination, the domestic scale plus frequent significant and motivated turns in the plot, defines a literary mode, which I do not hesitate to call realism. I use the term in a perfectly conventional way. If we broaden the scale ever so slightly, if the fiction is allowed to touch not a mere dozen people, but a fair number more, and if we loosen somewhat our rules about the kinds of characters that may appear, the combination I speak of can fairly be called one of the important ingredients of European realism. How does one sum up in a formula several centuries of the history of drama and of narrative fiction? Broadly speaking, realism, the realism we have in mind when we think of literature up to our time, is made up of three components. The first we could in general terms call description. Ancient rhetoric defines and prescribes a group of figures by which descriptions of objects (including persons) and events set these realities before the eyes of the audience, as though its members were actually witnessing them. The figures themselves consist of accumulations of circumstances supposed to attend the object described. The significance of these figures for realism or for realistic literature need not be stressed. It is enough to point out that Roland Barthes' «effet du réel», with its deconstructive twist, is the latest avatar of the ancient *enargeia* or *hypotyposis*.[12] Barthes, who knew and understood rhetoric very well, must surely have been aware of the ancestry of his concept. The second ingredient of realism is verisimilitude, our present theme. Verisimilitude is the principle that demands that the actions of the fictional characters match the audience's ideas and expectations about human behavior. The third factor in realism is the principle that the characters' actions are explainable on the basis not only of traits that are perennially human, but of those that have to do with a particular moment in history. Thus the deeds of a novel-character might make sense to us, if we understand that he is supposed to be a member of the rising middle class. This third element in realism obviously has nothing whatever to do with either Terence or Fernando de Rojas. We should, however, return to our second topic, and reflect how verisimilitude actually functions in texts we call realistic. Novelistic characters have the ring of truth in them, if we are allowed to see them acting not only in matters of large import, but of small, Trollope's Warden not only resigning his living out of principles of conscience, but acting in dozens of lesser circumstances, treating his rival with fairness and generosity, or even playing the cello for the pensioners. This wealth of represented actions which are recognizably human, this prodigality that is the mark of every classic novel is plainly one of the features that characterizes realism, as we know it. The note is not absent from either Terence or Rojas, different as their works may be from those of later writers. This aspect of realism in one way or another may actually be an inheritance from ancient comedy, and if we wish to show some solidarity between Rojas' great drama and those of Terence and Plautus, we must certainly take into account this capitally important dimension. And in fact, the quality is the most visible and conspicuous feature of *Celestina*. Every moment in the drama, every speech, has its logic. Sempronio's long harangue on mutability has as its burden two strains, «strike while the iron is hot», and more important, that if danger looms both he and Celestina should drop their plans to satisfy Calisto. The timid and cautious Sempronio is moved to speak at such length because of a careless remark of Celestina that novice lovers give no thought to the harm they can cause their retainers. Celestina herself in her first interview with Melibea speaks at length on the trials of old age. This is with malice aforethought: she wishes to bring home to Melibea the notion that youth and beauty are fleeting. We may continue in this vein at pleasure. There is scarcely a scrap of dialogue or bit of business which does not invite some sort of comment about mo-

---

[12] «L'Effet du réel», *Communications,* 11 (1968), 84-89.

tives, and it is in great part this richness, this thoroughly wrinkled surface, that makes the great tragicomedy what it is. We may observe finally that the old critical commonplace that *Celestina* is a realistic masterpiece is to this extent quite valid.

Is Rojas' great drama, then, simply modern? Obviously not, on many grounds. Even on the basis I have been speaking of, the supposed realism of *Celestina,* there may be limits to its forward-looking character. Indeed, we could reverse ourselves completely and assert that the *Tragicomedia* is a fictional text about characters who could not possibly exist in real life. The reader, incidentally, need not cavil at the expression «real life»; I believe that we have sufficiently hedged around the meaning of the word «realism» so that too much need not be claimed for the concept. «Real» characters may be flimsy merchandise, but I am thinking of genuine inverisimilitude. No genuine female pander would speak as Celestina does. Servants born in very mean circumstances like Pármeno would be unlikely to speak of *potentia* and *actus.* Sempronio's real-life analogue would not paraphrase the letters of the younger Seneca. Least of all would Areúsa's sisters in the real world be likely to lecture us on the folly of listening to popular opinion. In a word, the moralizing erudition that decorates the speeches of most of the characters in the play has nothing to do with plausibility. We have after all a term of contrast. The learned allusions are justified only in the case of Melibea herself, who, as we know, was a great reader, and who on her own admission drew the *exempla* in her speeches from books. But she is alone. The personae of the others are as unreal as three-dollar bills. None of this is news. I have in mind, however, a special sense in which old verisimilitude and new realism do not entirely match. Let us return to Donatus' commentary, which Rojas may have thought normative, and which may be an index to the way he and his contemporaries read Terence. As I have indicated, the commentator points out the motives of his characters in passages that at times come fast and frequent. In the *Eunuchus* Chaerea, now disguised as the eunuch, is in flight, but it is his bad luck to run into the courtesan Thais, in whose service he is supposed to be. He says «haereo», roughly, «I'm brought up short». [13] Donatus, taking into account the dialogue which follows, says that fear takes away Chaerea's judgment, but that reflection restores it. Thais, of course, is severe with the young man and threatens to punish him (850). The commentary says that she is in a position to act as she does because Chaerea was dressed as a eunuch and a slave. A further note observes that she is speaking ironically, «subtiliter», be-

[13] This is in line 848 in the play. My references to Donatus' commentary are sufficiently identified by the verse of the comedy in question. My notation of the verses henceforth will serve as references to the Latin original, to the English translation and to Donatus' comments. My text of the last is Wessner's, as in note 10.

case she knows that the man before her is not Dorus, but Chaerea. «Have you been trying to escape?», asks Thais. «Yes», answers Chaerea (851). He confesses readily, because he has no choice but to answer plainly and truthfully, Donatus says in effect. Thais' slave Pythia throws it in Chaerea's face that he raped a virgin, a free-born woman. «I thought she was a fellow slave» is his answer. His word, «conservam» (859), sends Pythia into a rage, witness her brief tirade. Quite in line, says Donatus, since Pythia is a *conserva* herself. Thais says to the young man that his impulsive act has spoiled all her plans, that she had hoped to restore the girl —the rape victim— to her family and so win some good will for herself (864-871). She is a sly one, says Donatus. She dares not mention marriage to the young man, but that is what is on her mind: she knows that he loves the girl and is gently pushing him into marrying her. Chaerea says himself that he loves Philomena, but in an overflow of good will confesses to Thais that he loves her too (882). Donatus comments trivially that the «quoque», «too», is appropriate, since he already loves someone else. This set of notes in the commentary is entirely typical. So also are the ones on another passage, this time from *Hecyra*. Phidippus has just found out that his daughter is pregnant. His wife Myrrina, who has known all along, fears her husband's anger, and says so in a soliloquy. They meet.

P: Here, Myrrina, I'm speaking to you.
M: To me, husband?
P: Your husband, am I? I wasn't sure you credited me with human feelings at all. If you'd ever thought of me as a husband, or even as a human being, woman, you wouldn't have made a fool of me with your goings on.
M: What have I done? (quibus)
P: Can you ask? Our daughter has had a baby. Well, have you nothing to say? Who's the father?
M: Is that a proper question for a father to ask? Gracious me, who on earth do you think but her husband?
P: I suppose so; as her father I can hardly think otherwise. What I can't understand is why you have been so anxious to conceal the birth from us all, especially when the birth was normal and at the right time (516-31).

These few lines are the basis for no fewer than six observations in the commentary about motives. Myrrina's distress expressed in the soliloquy is the result of an uneasy conscience. The innocent «quibus?» «What have I done?» is «mira calliditas», deep malice aforethought: Myrrina called to account defends herself by accusing. Phidippus' «Can you ask?» is appropriate: he is angry because she has asked a question when she very well knows the answer. When Myrrina says that of course the girl's husband is the father of the child, Phidippus once again is put on the defensive. «Sed dimiror» («What I can't understand») shows that Myrrina's sagacity has reduced her husband's anger to simple surprise or astonishment. When he further admits that the child was born at the proper time, he shows again that she has done her work well: she has no need to insist further on her daughter's innocence.

These remarks and the thousands of others like them in the Donatus commentary may range in value from the trivial to the reasonably pertinent; in no instance can we call them great criticism —that judgment would be irrelevant in any case. Taken as a whole their importance for literature and culture is immense. We need only imagine generations of students reading Terence, perhaps for the first time, being obliged on every page to look behind the surface of the narrative, being forced to comprehend each action and each saying as intentional, as fully human. The novice in letters who is taken on this trip would come to know a great deal about motives, perhaps even a great deal about life. Cicero's proposition that comedy was «an imitation of life, a mirror of custom, an image of truth» would not be an empty generalization for him: he would be able to vindicate it in plentiful detail. Most important of all, the practical man of letters, the writer, who has Terence-plus-Donatus as part of his training would already have taken a large first step. Having seen all the implications of the acts and speeches of all the Gnathos and Parmenos spun out fine for him, he would have had a very good idea of how to give plausibility and depth to the deeds of his own characters. *Celestina* may be unique, but a great deal of its substance and personality is already in Donatus' great text, or in something like it.

But exactly what contribution has the Terence commentary made? Let us look once again at our page of extracts. If we take counsel with our vulgar nineteenth-century prejudices about literature, we notice immediately that something is missing: we are struck by the fact that observations about character and characterization are never in the foreground. In the stratum of scholia and comments that I have been speaking of every detail of the play under discussion becomes plausible, every move gets traced to its human origins, but these observations are strictly local: scarcely ever are they related to the large traits of the individual personality. In Donatus psychological realism is in total and strict exile. We must be very clear what is at issue. In a set of comments in Donatus that I have not yet spoken of, character is indeed an important subject, and we can scarcely leave this set of remarks out of account. Sosia in the first scene of *Andria* speaks a *sententia* (61). It's legal, says Donatus: the speaker is a former slave, but the saying is in character, because it is proverbial. Gnatho in the *Eunuchus* introduces himself in a long speech (232). He shows himself a true parasite and his words express his corrupt character: so says the commentary. Of another scene in the same play in which we have an exchange between Gnatho and Thraso, Donatus says that it contains «assentationem parasiticam et stultitiam gloriosi militis» (391). Do all these remarks fall somewhere short of Henry James? They of course have nothing whatever to do with psychological analysis. Donatus is simply concerned with dramatic decorum. He takes as his starting-point a repertory of human types, the old man, the young lover, the courtesan, the braggart soldier, and so on, and judges the verisimilitude of the deeds of the characters and of their speeches on the basis of these types: this action is characteristic of an old man, that speech, of a flattering courtesan. We must not oversimplify this characterology: it has its subtleties. But we may be assured that it stays well within the realm of genera and species: within this system individuals become interesting only as they are associated with some kind of universal.

In Donatus there is simply nothing between these extremes. On one hand the local observation and on the other the noting of typical actions; the middle ground of character analysis, even in its most modest sense, is impossible to find. We could observe that students with a humanistic background would have at hand a remark of Horace that characters in a play should act consistently (*Ars poetica* 125-27). These lines might confirm what common sense adds to the observations in Donatus, that Phaedria or Chremes could not act at one moment in a way that was incompatible with what each did at another. Nothing in the commentary tells us that the career within the plays of a single character should not be logical or consistent. A more fundamental observation might be that the whole notion of individual character is riddled with ideology, and that by contrast the concept of personality implicit in Donatus is a reasonable and adequate one. After we have associated an individual with a class of some sort, what else is there to do but follow him and his reactions from one situation to the next, and the next, as though this were very nearly all one could observe about him? As our censorious maiden aunts used to say, that's life: one scene succeeds another, and their sum is everything we are. The very idea of a global individual personality, manifest in every detail of one's life, is a vague and elusive one. When someone attributes such a global character to an individual, real or fictional, one of two things happens: either the description becomes wooly, sentimental and moralizing, or else a sorry fatality takes over and the account inevitably spills over into genera and species, whether we like it or not.

So it would seem. But perhaps personality and character is not the whole issue. The old New Comedy is not simply or primarily a portrait gallery. What the elegant Terence of all the ancients gives us in his comedies is not merely verisimilitude of character, but, perhaps more important, verisimilitude of situation. This is surely what all the bits of commentary are about that I have spoken of. Why does Phormio speak here with such confidence? Why does Thais use indirection there? The

34

answer in both cases lies not only or principally in the individual nature of the speakers, but rather in the practical circumstances in which they are speaking. We may recall at this point Bataillon's reflections about Gaspar von Barth and his criticism of *Celestina*. The great French Hispanist's downgrading of the importance of character to the advantage of other factors has much the same sense that my remarks have. His text, the writings of von Barth, are a good witness: von Barth's humanism, the study of rhetoric, the study of poets, would have led him to much the same area we have been exploring, the world of grammarians, commentaries and their lore. Von Barth's verisimilitude is like Donatus' and like ours, and has more to do with circumstance than with the notes and characteristics of individuals.

Verisimilitude of situation is of course not unmodern. The most vulgar popular novel built along classical lines thrives on it. What is unmodern is the assumption that verisimilitude comes to full flower in character. Terence filtered through the comments of Donatus, the schoolbook of thousands, is our witness. This composite text stands as a warning that we should not read *Celestina* with modern eyes, that as I have remarked, its very genuine realism has its limits. Donatus' work and others like it should convince us that for the first author, for Rojas, and for *Celestina*'s first generations of readers character in our sense was not the show. The two great makers, if we understand matters fully, do give us an overwhelming impression of reality, but that reality does not include individuals endowed with unique personalities. *Celestina* is dialogic: I acknowledge my partial coincidence with Gilman and my debt to him (on many counts).[14] Characters take on plausibility as we see them in the presence of each other and in the web of circumstance they weave together with fortune. *Celestina,* in a word, gives us the verisimilitude of situation.

The representation of persons poses serious problems for the student of the *Tragicomedia,* and we must return to that large subject presently. For the moment let us observe that the Terence commentary of Donatus is in the class of texts that on one hand give a full and accurate account of ancient comedy, but which on the other lay down a statute broad enough to cover *Celestina*. Its particular function in my argument was to show that the general requirement that comedy be an imitation of life and a mirror of truth need not be an empty piece of piety, but that it could be made to refer to genuine and identifiable qualities in the comic text.

* * *

[14] STEPHEN GILMAN, *The Art of «La Celestina»* (Madison: Univ. of Wisconsin Press, 1957); the dialogic character of *Celestina* is a theme throughout the whole of Gilman's book.

Our investigation must now take a different direction. In the preceding section we were attempting to find definitions of comedy which Rojas might have been acquainted with, and to which his work in a general way did conform. In the pages that follow I shall take certain aspects of Rojas' actual practice which one might believe were distinctive and try to show that each of these has its precedent, that all belong in one way or another to the comic tradition. The definitive *Celestina* reaches out in many directions, but what needs to be shown is that for Rojas none of these initiatives was a violation of what he might have thought constituted comedy. Our documents, the body of texts that Rojas would have regarded as normative, consists of the following: the plays of Plautus and Terence, the Donatus commentary with its introductory essays, and the body of neo-Latin comedies which are usually called Humanistic. To this we must add certain bits of the lore of the liberal artist, which I shall identify in time; these, as we shall see, may have some bearing on the shape Rojas' tragicomedy took in its final version. My inclusion of the Humanistic comedies in my list of course requires some justification.

The reason they appear there can be broken down into two. In the first place, these fifteenth-century plays were his immediate model. *Celestina* is a humanistic comedy, differing formally from the other examples only in that it is written in the vernacular: this point has been made more than once, and it is unnecessary to argue the case again. But there is a complication. What exactly were Rojas and his predecessors copying? Did these plays constitute a separate genre for them? Would Rojas have assented readily to María Rosa Lida de Malkiel's judgment and said yes, indeed, I was writing a humanistic comedy? The question is not idle. It brings me to my second point. There is no reason why the authors of *Celestina* might not have thought of the Italian plays as comedies simply, and no reason either why their corpus of comic texts should not have included Paolo Vergerio and Aeneas Sylvius Piccolomini as well as Plautus and Terence. Let us return to the definitions of comedy aired in this study, the explicit ones in the introduction to Donatus' commentary, and the practical one in the body of the text: there is absolutely nothing in any of them that would not fit the fifteenth-century plays. We may make the same case for them that has already been made for *Celestina*. A modern reader may think that most of these Latin comedies are far removed from Plautus and Terence, but what their authors and contemporaries thought was essential to the species of the old plays might well be different from what we think. So also would what Rojas and his predecessors thought: that of course is the essential matter in this case. Add to this that in detail, in certain dramatic situations, but above all in language, the plays imitate Terence and even more Plautus, and the solidarity of these comedies with their ancient models would have seemed the more obvious to him. We could put the whole matter in modern

36

terms. The humanistic comedy is a reading, of sorts, of the old plays. It seems likely to me not only that Rojas so regarded them, but that that reading was also his reading.

Celestina is light-years away from its models. There are many reasons why one might agree with this proposition: there are many kinds of such reasons. We might have in mind the scope, the depth, in a word the ambition of the great drama, what it attempts and what it achieves. But what are we to say about formal matters? Is the *Tragicomedia* unique with regard to aspects of its form as it may be in other ways? I am asking once again if Rojas' work in fact violates the rules of comic genre, and further, whether its originality and greatness might not be precisely that it establishes new rules, that its author invented a new discourse, a new *écriture*. The answer will have to be partial and local. I shall examine in detail five aspects of *Celestina* which might tempt us to respond in the affirmative. These aspects all are bound up with qualities in the play which by general agreement would be considered splendid. The five aspects are the treatment of space, the style, or as I should say, the idiom of the speeches as accommodated much more to the person addressed than to the character of the speaker, dramatic irony, the dark side —the pathos, blood, the unhappy ending—, and finally the conception and development of character. The question of space first. On the face of it one would think there would be little to add to Lida de Malkiel's superb treatment of the subject (*Originalidad,* 149-68). In her subtle and judicious account of *Celestina* she asks us to imagine a plurality of places, Calisto's house, the street, Celestina's cottage and so on, but there is a flowing, or if we like, a kind of leakage between those places: we are, for example, asked to follow Sempronio and the old woman as they walk from her quarters to Calisto's house. There are paths and channels through which the separate places communicate. This, as Lida de Malkiel says, is quite the way space is organized in the humanistic comedies, although she is quick to point out that in this aspect both they and *Celestina* have medieval roots. In sum, the conception and treatment of space has much in it that separates it from the Roman plays. While all of this is quite true, there is a very different case that might also be made. What is remarkable about the Spanish text is how much it preserves of the New Comedy's sense of space. This parallel to some may seem far from obvious, and we must look at both sides of the comparison. Let us consider a few details of *Celestina* in which spatial relationships are significant. There are the asides, for example. The point may seem trivial, but a dramatic aside assumes that there is enough distance between the speaker and a second person on stage so that the latter need not hear him. In the case of the characteristic *Celestina* asides in which the speaker is overheard, but not understood, the distance is specified still

37

further: it must be short. The term of comparison would be the dialogue in certain medieval works, the *Libro de buen amor,* for example, in which the intervening space between the two speakers is not specified in any way at all. *Celestina* also has much more striking examples of scenes where spatial relationships are significant. One of the great ornaments of the first act is the sequence in the old bawd's house. As we recall, Sempronio overtakes the residents there at an embarrassing moment. Elicia is obliged to hide her lover of a season in a closet. She distracts Sempronio by pretending to be angry at his neglect. Time passes. Inevitably the ceiling creaks: «Who's upstairs?» asks the young man. «My lover», answers Elicia, with superb malice. «I'm going to see», he says, and we imagine him starting up the stairs. Only at the eleventh hour does Celestina step into the breach with a tantalizing bit of invented gossip which lures Sempronio away from his search. This astonishing and wonderful episode is a success on many counts. We could revive the theme of the «verisimilitude of situation». There is the artfulness of the two women, each plying very different tricks. There is the gullibility of Sempronio overtaking his initial suspicion. But all of the art of this scene presupposes a very determinate sort of space; Celestina's house has an outside: the unwelcome guest has to be admitted. There is a lower chamber, a stairway, and an infamous upstairs. Sempronio must wait outside, pass through the door and go part way up the stairs. Without this well-defined spatial basis, none of the events in the scene could happen, and the whole sequence would be impossible. Let us consider next the long double dialogue in Act VI, one of the glories of Rojas' work. There are four people speaking: Celestina, just returned from Melibea's house, Calisto, who receives her, and the two servants who listen and talk with each other. Again, a brilliant play of contrasting interests and intentions: Calisto distracted literally out of his mind by his anxiety over the outcome of Celestina's mission, the old woman herself, with her gilded but truthful account of what happened at Melibea's house, Pármeno, seeing malice in every move of the bawd, and the timorous Sempronio, trying to silence him. Now, we have four speakers, one more than Horace allows. How do we place four speakers? Are they in a row? in a square? The point is that if there are more than two, we have to place them somewhere: the third must form a triangle with the other two, or be between them, or on the side of one or the other. Two speakers pose no problem: they can whisper to each other at two inches' distance or shout at each other through bullhorns. We do not have to imagine them in any particular arrangement. But four we cannot leave dangling. Even if the text does not tell us exactly where each is standing, we must imagine them placed somewhere. In the case of *Celestina,* VI we get certain clues that are fairly clear. The two servants are presumably speaking in a low voice;

they must be at close quarters. The other pair must be at a moderate distance. Calisto hears little of the servants' talk, but the astute and interested Celestina does not miss a word, as we discover later. Pármeno and Sempronio of course hear everything the other two are saying. Rojas does not draw a map, but he does indicate certain areas with some clarity.

We could multiply examples of scenes like this. There is, for example, the fine one in which Melibea overhears her parents speak of her marriage. Episodes of this sort, in which we [...] a fairly determinate spatial arrangement, are among th[...] the whole tragicomedy. Without trying [...] ess that much of Celestina's standing [...] ds on just these passages. Is this whole[...] far back does it go? What you don't k[...] me, when I was young. What the authors of Celestina and [...] s of humanistic plays almost certainly did not know was the way the old theaters were arranged and what the conventions were that attended this layout. The New Comedies, Greek and Roman, were played on a stage that represented a street. There were more or less permanent structures that could serve as houses, two or perhaps three, that faced the street. There could be an altar. If the street was supposed to be in Athens, as was often the case, stage left was understood to lead to the center of town and stage right to the Piraeus. Actors' movements, therefore, were perfectly intelligible to the audience. They could enter the houses, they could walk from one house to the other, stop at the altar, arrive from the Agora, or if they had supposedly just landed from a sea journey, they could walk in from the port. Most important of all, there was the broad extent of the stage-street. Actors could in fact be at any distance from each other which might be appropriate, all the way from inches to the whole length of the stage.[15] My point in airing all of this material is that all these stage dispositions and conventions left very clear traces in the text of the old plays: even a reader who knew nothing of the ancient theater except for the actual words of the comedies would have no difficulty reading these traces. Where things happen is pretty well specified. We could make a little repertory of moments in Terence comparable to the one made of bits of the Celestina. Pamphilus and Davus are talking together: Simo comes on the scene and says, «I'm back to see what they're up to and what plans they're laying» (Andria, 404). He obviously does not see the two, and so must be at a certain distance. There is the very funny scene later in Andria between Davus, Mysis and Chremes. Davus has persuaded Pamphilus to agree to the marriage with Chremes'

---

[15] See GEORGE DUCKWORTH, The Nature of Roman Comedy (Princeton: Univ. Press, 1952), pp. 119, 121 ff., and R. L. HUNTER, The New Comedy, pp. 11 and 15.

daughter. His object was to convince Simo of his son's good will: as we recall, Simo has pretended to arrange such a marriage. But when the genuine wedding is actually in the wings, the slave must do what he can to keep it from taking place. He persuades Mysis to put the baby on Chremes' doorstep, and then, with Chremes present, pretends outrage at her act. In the course of the dialogue he obliges her to confess that the infant is Pamphilus' child by the Andrian woman. This broad melodrama has its effect: Chremes of course takes note and resolves to call off the wedding. But the victim in the scene is the simple Mysis, who throughout its length has not the faintest idea of what Davus is up to, and responds to his angry cries with words that are at times inappropriate (ll.740ff.). Once again, two and one: we have to place Davus and the girl close to each other and Chremes at a certain distance. This fine scene was conceived with a stage in mind and actors who would take their positions as the text demanded. The savor and the fun of the dialogue would be unintelligible without at least a spatial arrangement on an imaginary stage. In general terms, then, we could say that the disposition of place and space in *Celestina* is in great part the author's interpretation of Plautus and Terence with an essential part of the text missing, the stage conventions of ancient comedy.

Plainly un-Roman, as I believe, is the most pervasive quality of *Celestina,* the fact that the style, personality, the *ethos* of the individual speeches are determined more by the speaker's audience than by the personality of the speaker himself. We are obviously on Gilman's turf, once again (*Art,* p. 19). The trait, as I say, is unterentian. Neither is it characteristic of Plautus' work, although the latter's does pose more problems in this sense than Terence's. Terence will be our term of comparison. The accommodation of the idiom of the speech to the listener and not the speaker is something that is likely to happen most frequently, perhaps, when the latter is trying to deceive. Deception, needless to say, constitutes a large ingredient in the plots of the ancient comedies, but in point of fact style and idiom do not come much into the picture there. By and large style is fairly uniform in Terence: there are shadings, but as a whole the range is narrow. Character, situation and speech are differentiated by what the people say, and not by the tone in which they say it. One could remark that for many writers of fiction and drama this is a system that is entirely effective. Rojas and his predecessors, as we know, take a different course. Idiom is everything, as I tried to show in my introduction, and idiom is determined by the setting in which a speech is delivered. The accommodation to the listeners through idiom is everywhere. Often it has to do with dissimulation, but sometimes it does not. It is not wholly lacking from any speech in the drama, not even the most insignificant.

I shall let these generalizations stand without documenting them. Their truth seems to me to be obvious, and indeed, I am not the first to give utterance to it. There is, however, one narrower phenomenon which does deserve comment, a feature which has surely caught the attention of nearly every reader of *Celestina,* erudite or not. This is the eloquent speech, the utterance of which is sententious, moralizing, learned, the building-block so characteristic of both parts of the *Tragicomedia,* Rojas' and his predecessor's. As we know, the presence in the work of this particular strain has been viewed in several ways. The sententious component in this mix was to María Rosa Lida de Malkiel an element of stylization comparable to the verse in Shakespearean drama (*Originalidad,* p. 333). The same factor was to the mind of Spitzer an important part of the rhetoric of the work globally, the rhetoric of the author's voice and of his message.[16] But as concerns the matter of weighty eloquence as a whole, it is Gilman who has the most pertinent things to say.[17] Eloquence is a function of dialogue. The *Art of «La Celestina»* does not, as I recall, deal in principle or in isolation with the learned speech in its rhetorical aspect, but it does so in fact, always reducing this note to its function within the dialogue. What to my mind needs to be pointed out is that generally the speech composed in a weighty style is the eminent case of the utterance designed to produce some abnormal effect in the listener, that rarely does a character become eloquent and moralizing without some sort of malice aforethought, broad or discreet. Whenever the speaker pulls out the stops, so to speak, we can be fairly sure that there is some intention afoot not wholly in line with the plain sense of the speech. There are striking exceptions, of course. Sempronio's long mutability piece in Act III is not learned and eloquent because he means in any way to manipulate Celestina. It is instead a disproportionate response to her remark that lovers sometimes love to the peril of their servants: Sempronio lacks courage of any sort and his utterance is first and foremost a reaction to her words. We recall Gilman's remark about logic and sentiment in *Celestina.* Likewise Pleberio's speech at the end of the play has nothing of calculation in it. It on one hand expresses the speaker's grief at the death of his daughter, and on the other is quite simply the author's voice, giving us in a general way the sense of the whole work. But these pieces are exceptional. Normally when a speaker in the play takes a learned and moral tone, he has an eye on his audience, not infrequently a malicious eye. Obvious examples are everywhere in the work. «Goodness didn't have nothing to do with it», Mae West said. There is Sempronio's tirade on honor and liberality at the beginning of

---

[16] LEO SPITZER, «A New Book on the *Celestina*», *Hispanic Review,* 25 (1957), 1-25, at pp. 8-9.
[17] See especially the chapter in *The Art* on «The Art of Style», pp. 17-55.

Act II, recommending a course of action which is not at all honorable and hardly liberal. There are Celestina's remarks on poverty and old age and stoical resignation addressed to Melibea in Act IV: though they do not say so, they are plainly meant to give a color of dignity to the disreputable old woman and force her listener to reflect that youth and beauty are fleeting. In these particular utterances and in others like them there are bushels of plain falsehood on the part of the speakers. We may of course find blander examples. There is Celestina's magisterial tone to Sempronio as they go together for her second visit to Calisto:

> El propósito muda el sabio; el necio persevera. A nuevo negocio, nuevo consejo se requiere. No pensé yo, hijo Sempronio, que assí me respondiera mi buena fortuna. De los discretos mensageros es hazer lo que el tiempo quiere... (V.15)

The old woman wishes to give a look of legitimacy to her unsavory course of action, and also to maintain an air of superiority over Sempronio, even though in both estate and moral character they are equals. Finally let us consider this throw-away speech in Act IV. Melibea has curtly dismissed Celestina, but the latter makes it clear she has more to say. Say on, says the young woman:

> Di, madre, todas tus necessidades, que si yo las pudiere remediar, de muy buen grado lo haré, por el passado conocimiento y vezindad, que pone obligación a los buenos. (IV.48)

The sentence is marked by its fair length, its somewhat complicated syntax, and above all by the commonplace expressed: «conocimiento y vezindad ponen obligación a los buenos.» What does its formal tone express? A certain coldness and distance, perhaps, a warning to Celestina, a person of no great good repute, not to speak lightly. I cite this tiny example to call attention to the pervasiveness in *Celestina* of high speech plus indirection. The old woman's perverse counsels to Pármeno in Act I, and many other passages, including some I have commented on, display the combination in the plain light of day, but it can also find its way into the tiniest nooks and corners of the text where one would not expect to come upon it.

I am impelled first of all to make some remarks about diction and register in *Celestina*. Sententious style, as I have said, is often pressed into service when the authors wish their characters to show a certain duplicity. These moments, as one would think, should be unique dramatic situations, and yet the high style in the play is absolutely uniform. I, of course, distinguish between style and idiom: idiom varies constantly within the text, whereas style is of two or three kinds each undifferentiated as to speaker or situation. The noble voice appropriated by Celestina is not very unlike the noble voice in Pármeno's mouth, or

Sempronio's. Only Calisto is distinctive in this regard: his eloquent style is extravagant and hyperbolic, diction decorous in a distraught lover. With this one exception style does not distinguish estate, moral character, individual psychology or even situation. The term of contrast here is Elizabethan drama, in which base characters do not speak in verse, and indeed each single one may have his distinctive rhythm, diction and repertory of figures of speech.

A more pertinent observation I must make is about decorum in *Celestina*. Having in mind not only the passages in high sententious style, but all in which style or idiom or both are determined by their expected effect on the listener and not by the sentiments of the speaker, I must insist that there is nothing new here: this feature is not distinctive to the *Tragicomedia*, nor is it an invention of its authors. It is envisioned in ancient rhetoric. Decorum, as the old authors state, is of more than one kind. The orator must speak decorously with respect to his own person, to be sure, but also with regard to other factors, the occasion, for example, and most significantly, the character of his audience. Rhetoric always is the grid. There is little in the design and detail of *Celestina* whose place and existence are not in some way prepared by rhetoric. But is this decorum of the listener in our text a novelty in drama? If we frame the question as broadly as this, the answer is trivial: no, obviously not. Would it indeed be possible to compose a play so completely lacking in dramatic illusion that its characters would never have to adjust their remarks to their hearers? But if we take the narrower case, the eloquent moralizing speech as a grandstand play, the question of originality is real. The feature is characteristic enough so that it is possible to trace its history. It is, as I believe, not ancient. But it can be found everywhere in the Humanistic Comedy. An obvious and simple example is supplied by Herotes' speech near the beginning of Vergerio's fine play *Paulus*. The spineless student, who gives the work its title, has wasted months and years at the university, but suddenly announces to his servant that he means to turn over a new leaf and study in earnest. Herotes asks why he has taken this resolve so suddenly. «Don't ask», the young man answers, «my mind is made up.» The servant's next speech begins with a frank aside, «ego pervertam omnia», and continues warning Paulus that on the eve of feast days his new zeal could be taken for either poverty or miserliness. Follow moderation in all things, he says, and depend on your native wit, a gift more precious than all the wisdom that is in books:

> ... numquam tibi auctor ero ego,
> Ut te excrucies. Modum in omnibus rebus
> Servari aiunt nostri philosophi. Non es tu,
> Cui quaerendus sit ex studio nummus,
> Servent superi modo, quae domi sunt,
> Quemve gravare possit impensa longior.

Ego, si detur optio mihi, nolim plenus esse litterarum
Ita raro summae litterae cum summa prudentia coeunt.
Tu, vero, quoniam abundas innata disciplina, quam
Non dant scolae, ubique clarus vel sine libris
Eris[18].

Passages like this are not hard to find in the fifteenth-century Latin plays. In the famous *Poliodorus* of Johannes de Vallata the Celestina-like character assumes this mode in a speech I have quoted elsewhere.[19] This fact is interesting, if we consider the claims that have been made for this text as a source for *Celestina*.[20] The eloquent moralizing speech uttered with indirection, the feature that is so prominent in our Spanish *tragicomedia,* therefore is not an original pattern there. Indeed if we were setting out to prove that *Celestina* was of a piece with the Humanistic Comedy, we might well cite passages of this type as evidence. That is obviously not what we are about in the present instance.

At bottom, our quarry here is the Romantic notion that originality and greatness are everywhere and always synonymous. Here is a structural feature in *Celestina* applied in a fashion that we cannot but admire: in large part the great *Tragicomedia* is for us those mountainous speeches of Celestina, of Sempronio, said with malice aforethought. If these fine tirades move us, as they must, their underlying structure must have represented a spontaneous move on the part of the author, his inspiration come to full flower. And yet this is not so. Brilliant as these speeches are, their premise is not only not new to Rojas or his predecessor. Its application is actually a positive sign, a mark that identifies their work as a genuine comedy, well within the norms of the comic genre.

Dramatic irony is another structural feature of *Celestina* which is bound up with qualities we admire in the work. Surely some of its greatest moments are those in which the audience is aware of things of which the characters themselves are ignorant. I would remark especially that dramatic irony artfully exploited is a mark of the work of Rojas, the second author. The post-1499 sections of his drama are generally remarkable for the far-reaching initiatives he takes with his own work, but none is more moving than the scene in which Pleberio and his wife discuss a possible marriage for their daughter. He is concerned for her honor:

ninguna vertut ay tan perfeta que no tenga vituperadores y maldizientes. No ay cosa con que mejor se conserve la limpia fama en las vírgines, que con temprano casamiento. (XVI.6)

[18] *Teatro goliardico dell'Umanesimo,* ed. Vito Pandolfi & Erminia Artese (Milano: Lerici, 1965), pp. 58, 60.

[19] JOHANNES DE VALLATA, *Poliodorus, comedia humanistica desconocida,* ed. J. M. Casas Homs (Madrid: CSIC, 1953), pp. 207-08. I quote this text in the next chapter.

[20] Casas Homs, in his introduction to *Poliodorus,* airs the question of influence.

But he cares also for her gratification in marriage. She should be the one to choose her future husband:

> Pues, ¿qué te parece, señora muger? ¿Devemos hablarlo a nuestra hija, devemos darle parte de tantos como me la piden, para que de su voluntad venga, para que diga cuál le agrada? Pues en esto las leyes dan libertad a los ombres y mugeres, aunque estén so el paterno poder, para elegir. (XVI.19)

At the moment he is speaking, Melibea is inches away, though unseen to him, and hears everything the parents say. Her love affair with Calisto is at this point well under way and for this reason what she hears is deeply and utterly distasteful to her. Her mother Alisa hardly makes matters easier, when she denies that Melibea is in any position to choose a husband. Her innocence makes this unfeasible: «¿Y piensas qué sabe ella qué cosa sean ombres, si se casan, o qué es casar? ¿O que del ayuntamiento de marido y muger se procreen los hijos?» (XVI.20). At this point Melibea implores Lucrecia to somehow get her parents off the painful subject: «interrúmpeles sus alabanças con algún fingido mensage, si no quieres que vaya yo dando bozes como loca, según estoy enojada del conceto engañoso que tienen de mi inorancia» (XVI.22).

The dramatic irony in *Celestina* has been discussed abundantly by María Rosa Lida de Malkiel, and there is little that needs to be added to her account. As she reminds us, the unknowing character observed by the knowing audience is almost the normal state of things in plays by Plautus and Terence. The «importance of being mistaken» is the mainspring of the plot of many of these plays.[21] As Lida de Malkiel also points out, dramatic irony is a pattern the *Tragicomedia* shares with the Roman comedy, but not with the Humanistic (*Originalidad,* pp. 250-64). The subtle grammarians and scholars who composed these plays apparently did not find this narrative and dramatic device in the ancients anything worth copying. Both these facts are significant, the Roman-Castilian coincidence, and the Roman-Italian divergence. The conception of comedy on all three fronts is what is interesting, the broad statute for the genre that permits these variations. What about the Roman Celestinesque side of this triangle? Calisto is standing at the closed door of Melibea's house: the two are conversing, unseen to each other. She hears voices in the street and fears for his safety. He reassures her: «Señora, no temas, que a buen seguro vengo. Los míos deven de ser, que son unos locos y desarman a cuantos passan, y hüiríales alguno.» Melibea asks: «¿Son muchos los que traes?» He answers, «No, sino dos; pero aunque sean seis sus contrarios, no recebirán mucha pena para les quitar las armas y hazerlos hüir, según su esfuerço» (XII.54-55). At the very moment he is extolling the courage of his servants, Pármeno and Sempronio are

---

[21] The phrase is the title of a heading in DUCKWORTH, Ch. 6.

expressing to each other unnatural cowardice, and are saying they will run at the first sign of danger; as we know, this dialogue takes up most of the scene. What is un-Roman about this sequence? To my mind, only one thing, its moral seriousness. In an ancient comedy, in a situation like this one in *Celestina,* the play of cross-purpose would be simply amusing, but here graver matters are involved, the complete lack of courage or loyalty on the part of the servants, and the hyperbolic style and total failure of judgment on the part of the lovesick Calisto. In a word, the difference is material. As a formal pattern the irony has nothing in it that would differentiate it from the irony of Plautus or Terence.

This in turn might show that Rojas need not have thought of a scene like this as a breach of the comic code. Let us look at another dramatic moment late in the play. How do we find out that Pármeno, Sempronio and Celestina are all dead? Sosia has witnessed the execution of the servants and comes to Calisto's house with the news. Tristán sees him approaching the house. We may gather from the boy's soliloquy that the other pair of servants has been killed, but he, of course, has no idea what has happened. His description of Sosia is humorous. Here is most of the speech:

> Quiero baxarme a la puerta, por que duerma mi amo sin que ninguno le impida, y a cuantos le buscaren se le negaré.—¡O, qué grito suena en el mercado! ¿Qué es esto? Alguna justicia se haze o madrugaron a correr toros. No sé qué me diga de tan grandes bozes como se dan. De allá viene Sosia, el moço de espuelas. El me dirá qué es esto. Desgreñado viene el vellaco. En alguna taverna se deve aver rebolcado, y si mi amo le cae en el rastro, mandarle á dos mil palos; que, aunque es algo loco, la pena le hará cuerdo. Parece que viene llorando. (XIII.9-11)

The pathos of the moment is heightened by the light tone of the speech, precisely, and by our knowledge that the bad news is going to take Tristán completely by surprise. The distinction here in this case is the linking of the dramatic irony to a pathetic situation. And once again we may observe that what is particularly Celestinesque and un-Roman is not in principle irony in itself, but the dramatic situation to which it is joined. The parallelism in this sense to the situation posed by the scene at Melibea's door is close, and it is significant. But there is more. Rojas' solidarity with the ancients is clearly signalled in the text. Tristán's speech is simply a Plautine soliloquy: it is a slave's speech, laced with humorous references to drunkenness and beatings. We have here the eminent case of tradition and the individual talent: the author is obviously marking his text as an imitation of Terence and Plautus just at the moment he is differing from them. But it is surely not overinterpreting to observe that since this difference is not formal, it is one more possibility exploited within the range of what for Rojas constitutes comedy.

To this point in our examination of the comic, or comedic, *Celestina* it has been possible to reduce our text to the norms of its genre. The great work may be a rogue among comedies, but on the basis of our tests to date we are still out of trouble: the play is well within the law. In one conspicuous area, however, there is a genuine violation, one that cannot be argued away. This is the drama's represented violence: as we know very well, the end of the play leaves us with no fewer than five characters who have met unnatural deaths. In the face of this grim state of affairs one might begin to wonder why Rojas wished to call the sixteen act play a *comedia*. Needless to say, neither the statutes nor the practice of the ancients condones such Jacobean happenings in a comedy. We recall that Diomedes and others thought that the comic plot should not include threats to life, much less its actual destruction. In the ancient plays themselves violent death is never in the foreground. But blood and death are not the only challenges to comic integrity in the *Celestina*. What about the unhappy ending, violence aside? And what about the pathos, and the moral seriousness? Do these elements have any sanction in precept or precedent? Is their presence in any way justifiable within a supposed comedy?

Once again, we must scrutinize the comic corpus. None of the plays of Plautus or Terence has an unhappy ending, but two humanistic comedies do, the *Paulus* of Paolo Vergerio and the *Philogenia* of Ugolino da Pisa.[22] So far, so good. If Rojas knew either or both of these works, or others like them, and if he considered such plays comedies, then the end of *Celestina* is less of an anomaly than it would be otherwise. The issue of the moral tone is more complicated. By convention and by precept the New Comedy is supposed to be a guide to living, and the actual plays have been praised for their usefulness in teaching morals. But a hasty comparison of any work by Terence with *Celestina* makes it clear that the moral conflicts in the latter are much more serious. The handful of passages I cited lately are cases in point: the deep folly of Calisto, his inability to judge his servants' character, their own faithlessness and cowardice are quite unlike anything in the old texts. In this whole case, as in the matter of the unhappy ending, the humanistic comedies may supply the link. In each of the two plays I have mentioned the final bad circumstance is brought about by the malice of one character. In *Paulus* the vicious servant from the very first does everything to distract Paulus from his studies and to make him waste his substance on the easy life. At the end we discover how deliberate this program is. Herotes tells us plainly that he is in the business of ruining young students: some he has served have been reduced to beggary, and it is clear that Paulus himself is to be the next victim. Herotes' ill-will is impressive, and it is distinctive. There is little in Terence or Plautus that in any way resembles him.

---

[22] This play is in Pandolfi and Artese, pp. 171-285.

Thoroughly vicious characters in the old plays are much less elaborately wicked. They are type characters; they normally belong to vicious professions, pander, slave-merchant, and the audience is plainly meant to expect no good to come from them. They are evil by routine, and the complicated malice of Herotes is wholly alien to them. But not at all alien to the *Tragicomedia*. Celestina, whose deliberation is almost total, is Herotes' sister; Sempronio and Pármeno, faithless and cowardly, but full of self-interest, are his near kin. I am of course speaking not of the subtlety of the presentation of all of these —Herotes is well-drawn in any case— but of the kind of malice they display, deliberate and particular.

Much the same can be said of the evil character in Ugolino's magnificent *Philogenia*, in this case not a servant, but a lover of high station. Epiphebus begins infatuated with the gentle but senseless heroine. At the end of a broadly-played seduction scene he not only wins her, but persuades her to leave her parents' home. Once gone, she cannot return: the respectable and small-minded pair will not have her back. Her existence during most of the play ia a *via crucis* from one house to another, and, as we learn from the dialogue, she learns promiscuity during the course of this adventure. Epiphebus, needless to say, soon loses interest in her, and ends by settling her on a coarse and repulsive peasant. He pretends that her marriage is to be a convenient front, and that he means to continue seeing her, but he is in fact abandoning her. The audience can measure the heartlessness of everything Epiphebus does by contrasting it to Philogenia's good qualities, which are many. She is frail, but fundamentally decent. She lacks sense, but in an astonishing moment of insight confesses as much. She is not vicious: a priest at one point helps her examine her conscience, and finds her innocent of all the great sins but one: this sin he dismisses as easily pardoned. We are severe with Epiphebus principally because he has taken advantage of her frailty: his adventure with her brings her terrible ill fortune which she does not in any way deserve. His malice also is plainly on a different scale from that of the pardonable frailties depicted in the old plays, impetuosity in the young, unreasonable severity in the old, artfulness and seductiveness in courtesans. Even the panders and slave merchants seem less destructive: their vice is so generalized that we hardly think of them as being wicked in one particular course of action. *Philogenia* is also materially unlike *Celestina*, but we can say of both that the moral judgments they ask us to make are deeper and more far reaching than anything Plautus and Terence demand of us.

We are supposed to feel pity for the unfortunate and ill-treated Philogenia. Her situation is desperate. Here, of course, we are on very different ground. Pathetic situations are not at all lacking in the old comedies. To be sure, the scale is broad, and most of the unhappy circumstances presented in them fall well short of the one in which we find Ugolino's heroine. But some come close. There is the one ancient tragicomedy, so called. Plautus uses the term humorously, but the tragic strain in *Amphitrion* is not negligible. The hero cannot possibly know that his wife has been faithful to him, and she for her part cannot possibly know that her child is not by him. It is only when Jupiter reveals himself as the true father that the terrible crisis passes. The god's trick is literally a blessing in disguise, and we know from the start that things will turn out well, but in another play of Plautus we have no such assurance: the comic convention obviously counts for something, but within the dramatic illusion nothing tells us with certainty that things will end happily. Lesbonicus in *Trinummus* overshoots every mark. He has wasted his father's substance completely, to the point of selling his house and leaving his sister without a dowry. More pathetic still is the lot of Pleberio and Alisa at the end of *Celestina*; this is, of course, the real point. We may think their lot unique, but nothing in the practice of comedy writing, ancient or modern (to Rojas), excludes even this large bundle of pathos.

* * *

The final section of this chapter will be given over to the question of character and characterization. The problem I wish to deal with is a plain paradox: generations of modern readers have seen in *Celestina* a gallery of full and rounded individual characters, and yet the poetic norms that Rojas and his predecessor would have known seem only to have provided for types. Now, the very idea of characterization is a broad one, as I have tried to show; it includes many strains and, as I believe, not a little confusion. We could remark here that in one sense we are already well into our discussion. Morals constitute an important element in character, and to the extent that we have alluded to the moral issues raised by the actions in our play, we have taken a large step into our subject. How often it is that readers declare a fictional character real and lifelike, when in fact all that has happened in the text is that he has made an important moral decision. The moral dimension in character, as we should stress, is on the universal or typical side of our paradox: ethics has to do with norms, and norms, however subtle or complex, are by definition universal.

My discussion will be divided into two parts: first I shall air some ideas about characterization in general, and then test the notion that the characters in *Celestina* are not meant to represent individuals, but types differentiated.

Gilbert Ryle once wrote some eloquent lines about winks.[23] A wink

---

[23] Paraphrased in CLIFFORD GEERTZ, *The Interpretation of Cultures* (New York: Basic Books, 1973), pp. 6-7.

4'

in his view cannot be simply a physiological happening or a reflex: a wink that is not deliberate is not a wink. There is a story told of Beethoven. An admirer once asked, pointing to the score, «What were you thinking of when you composed that immortal music?» The composer paused and then said, also pointing to the score, «I was thinking that». Soul, Ryle says, more or less, is in human actions, essential and intrinsic to them, and soul is nowhere else.[24] Ryle's term is, of course, mind, but my substitution is not an accident. The mental act is in the wink; it is not before it or somehow parallel to it. Beethoven's act of composition is complete and sufficient to itself: it is intentional, but the intention is not prior to it or in any way separate from it.

We understand others, and we understand fictional characters, because we are consciousness and so are they, either really or in imagination. So one might say. The loaded word in this utterance is «understand». It connotes something global, one soul penetrating to the very heart of another: «I understand Mary Ellen» means that I intuitively possess her essence, everything she is. All that is wrong. Separate human acts are indeed immediately comprehensible: we can for a fact recognize a wink as a wink. Understanding Mary Ellen is another matter. We must recall as many of her acts as we can and then we may believe that we see certain significant patterns: we make a set of judgments. My own self-awareness, so to speak, is not the instrument that I use to get to the essence of Mary Ellen. In fact, my knowledge of self is knowledge of the very same kind as my knowledge of her: on all the evidence I judge that I am such and such a kind of person. If I know more about myself than I do about her, it is simply that I am better documented: I am in a position to know and remember the things that I have done much better than I am to know what she has done (Ryle, pp. 155 ff.).

Let me remind the reader of everything I have said about Terence, Donatus, verisimilitude and the essence of comedy. What I should like to suggest here is that some of the things the ancients said about fiction and fictional characters have philosophical dignity and are perennially useful. Understanding a fictional character is in some instances not greatly different from understanding a real person. Donatus' line-by-line and action-by-action commentary is a good approach to Terence's characters and a similar procedure would be an excellent line to take with Nature's. Limitations on the scope of this proposition would have to be on the side of literature; not every mode of fiction is susceptible to Donatus' procedure, but in general terms his approach may well be widely applicable to life.

The word «characterization» is a semantic omnibus: it can mean

---

[24] RYLE, *The Concept of Mind* (New York: Barnes and Noble, 1949), passim: a fundamental theme of this book.

many different things. As concerns our special field, the authors of *Celestina*, their forbears and their commentators ancient and less ancient, we must distinguish between two senses. By the commonest and most vulgar usage, characterization is a collection of general statements: «George is loyal, trustworthy, brave, clean, reverent» or «Olga is tough, self-reliant, intelligent, resourceful». The list can be as long, as subtle, as paradoxical, as full of qualifying clauses as one likes: that is up to the author or his commentator. The list can appear in various forms and in various settings. As I suggest, it is not out of place in the mouth of a critic: Professor Smith puts down the *Tragicomedia* and declares that Celestina is sagacious, masterful, intelligent, malicious, and so on. The author himself can supply the list: if he is a novelist, he may serve it up under his own authority, but if he is a dramatist, he can put it into the mouth of a chorus, a prologue or, indeed, another character, and failing all that he can write an elaborate stage direction or rubric. But then he may not set the list down anywhere. It may be simply inside his head. In this case he will manage the character's career through the text in such a way that the reader can easily reconstruct the list on his own. Sam is cowardly: there is instance *a,* instance *b,* and instance *c.* The list of generalities is always an abstraction: this is not really a tautology. In the case of a real person it is a selection, more or less arbitrary, from the infinite store of propositions that could be made about him. Much the same can be said of a fictional character, if the text has a big enough supply of information about him. But beyond that, the items on the list are themselves abstractions: a general statement leaves out particulars by definition and the genuine character is made up of precisely a succession of particulars. One can only claim a first-hand reference for one's generality, if one has a systematic psychology or physiology. Don Quixote is choleric. This means he has a particular bodily disposition: many people can have this disposition, but our proposition attaches the quality to a single subject.

The second sort of characterization is the one I have already devoted so much space to. The author, initially at least, is concerned with making his character act credibly in one situation: he must so write his text that a particular wink comes out really a wink. To be sure, all the acts of a character put together in succession may have a certain logic and coherence to them, but that coherence may be one of many different kinds. The author may, for example, want his creature to be an unreasonable man, whose actions are incomprehensible to his family and friends. In any case I should emphasize that this logic is by no means necessarily reducible to our famous list: our character may be perfectly comprehensible to us and still be irreducible to the sort of formula the list implies.

There are two observations I must make about our two species of

51

characterization. First, both have to do with generalities, with universals. In the case of the list this is obvious, but in the case of the step-by-step characterization, it may be less so. What we must consider is this. Significance is common: a wink that cannot possibly or hypothetically be recognized is simply not a wink. Sempronio gives us his tirade on mutability because he is afraid: if we cannot recognize that fear as a possible motive in that situation, or the long speech as a plausible reaction, then Rojas' labor is in vain. I am not here speaking of absolutes: norms of sociability, norms of plausibility may and do change. That does not alter their status as universals, single norms covering a multiplicity of individual cases. I shall have much to say in time about such universals. My second observation has to do with the relationship between the two kinds of character drawing. It is this: the list, the general view of what a character is like, does not write a line of a play or work of fiction beyond itself. The author must put him into action on the first page, then on the second and third, and the most detailed and exquisitely constructed list will not spare him that labor. In other words, successive characterization is a job no poet within our mode can avoid, no matter how completely and perfectly he understands his character globally. Consider the constraint that Horace places on composers of tragedy, that the old characters should be presented the way tradition dictates, that Achilles should have such characteristics and so Orestes and Medea (*Ars poetica,* 119-27). We must still invent the first scene and find plausible things for our characters to do, and then we must go on to the second, and to the third. The plastic arts give us a good analogue. Supposing that a sixteenth or seventeenth-century painter is doing the Return from the Flight into Egypt. He must work within limits: Joseph must be old and grave, Mary, beautiful and virginal, Jesus, a perfect child. But how is the artist going to pose the three? Who is going to be looking at whom? Is Jesus going to be holding Mary's hand, looking up at her lovingly? The richness of a superb Rubens lies in great part in just these determinations, and the rules that he works within do not excuse him from making them.

Global characterization and successive characterization are in principle two quite different things. Most fictional texts have elements of both, although, as we should note, Gilman conceives the possibility of a work with only one, the successive (*Art,* p. 57). If there are both, how may they be distributed? Let us start with the two extreme cases. First, let us suppose that the character is not allowed to do anything in the whole length of the text that is not in the global account. Sam is cowardly and he is sentimental. Very well: we shall not invent any action for him in our play that does not show his cowardice or his sentimentality or both. Global and successive coincide. At the other extreme we can picture the global account as having no connection at all with the character's actions,

52

or with the successive account. This second possibility may seem hard to imagine in a real text. But I must confess that my deep irritation with *Brideshead Revisited* rests in great part on the fact that Sebastian's mother is put together in just this way. We are told that her very existence is a curse to all those close to her, especially to Sebastian, and yet we never actually see her being manipulative or possessive or acting in any way that would explain, for example, Sebastian's alcoholism.

This distribution of global and successive is the subject of the rest of this study. We are dealing with what seems to me to be a paradox. On one hand the characters in *Celestina* are to many readers exceedingly lifelike and individualized, but on the other everything that literary history tells us obliges us to see them under genera and species. The situation is of course not unique. There is even a kind of melodrama that develops. Philologists do their best with an old text: they explain what they can. But then armies of offended readers come on the scene, and there are accusations of insensibility and heartlessness: their *Hamlet* or their *Inferno* is violated. Characterization in *Celestina* may be just such a battleground, and I am proposing my views about global and successive as a possible peace treaty. There is no denying that Sempronio, Celestina, and even Lucrecia are beautifully conceived: the fine-spun web of motivation throughout the length of the text is of course one of its glories. What I wish to suggest is that the global component in the make-up of some of the characters, however important or fundamental, is relatively small: to understand that Calisto conforms to a type may be essential to an accurate reading of the play, but for all of that, his *differentiae* are exceedingly interesting in themselves and to a great extent he is memorable on their account. The corollary that I would draw is that to point out the generic in one or another of the *Celestina* characters is in no sense to violate them: the sensibility of the ordinary intelligent reader need not be offended.

The old texts talk about types. Evanthius praises Terence, because in the main his characters conform to the laws of *habitus, aetas,* and *officium* (III.4). The grammarian does add, reasonably, that the few breaches of decorum in Terence are effective and fundamentally true to life. His occasional good prostitute is a case in point. Donatus, as we have seen, is constantly pointing out actions of Terence's characters that conform to the types they represent, this saying, as appropriate to a slave, that act, to a parasite. The first observation we must make is that the types in *Celestina,* to the extent that there are such, are not the same as the ones in Terence. One might indeed insist that the two authors of the tragicomedy do observe the laws regarding *habitus, aetas,* and *officium,* just as Terence said to, but that their conformity yields different results. Their idea of a lover is hardly like his; the prostitutes are entirely

53

different. The *trotaconventos* has no analogue at all in Terence and Plautus. Rojas presents no parasites; his servants do not spin out elaborate plots, as do Terence's. I should suggest further that in some cases we might speak not of types, but of broad motives. Certain characteristics of age might be shared by Celestina and Pleberio; youthfulness is not the young lover's monopoly: it is also significant that Pármeno is young. I am obviously not thinking of two characters of the same type, as the two young lovers in *Andria* or, indeed, the two servants in *Celestina*. I mean, of course, that it might be suitable to think of portmanteau characters in our drama, figures that combine two or even more separate motives. *Celestina,* if it is a comedy, is a rogue comedy, as I have said, and one of the ways in which it shows its independence is that its conception of character is much less systematic than that of the ancients.

Calisto, wonderfully individualized as he is, is nevertheless the most perfectly typical character in the play. He is a distraught lover: he is in many ways quite of a piece with Chrétien's Lancelot and other medieval lover-heroes. As Otis H. Green and others have noted, the young man is suffering from *hereos,* lovers' malady:[25] the play of his imagination ocupies much of his life, and his judgments about the outer world miss their mark. He is moody, by turns very sad and very happy. All of these observations have been made before, and there is no need to go into great detail. It is remarkable how little that we know about him exceeds the pattern. He awakens once, not knowing at all what time of day it is. He writes verse. His judgment fails. As we have seen, he has not the faintest idea of what moves Pármeno and Sempronio: he declares them loyal and brave at the very moment when their cowardice is at its most scandalous. How afflicted is he? At one point Sempronio seriously fears for Calisto's life: the servant reflects that if his master dies, he the survivor is by law the prime suspect for murder. His actual love for Melibea exceeds the bonds of reason and even of religion. Our list could continue. Every scene in which he appears gives us one more look at our typical fool for love.

Rojas on one occasion allows Calisto to come to his senses. After the first night of love we see him for the first time taking full note of his desperate situation, his two servants dead, his honor undone. In his mind he rails against the judge who put Pármeno and Sempronio to death, but afterwards acknowledges that the judge acted fairly. He then launches complaints against God himself and Nature who keep him from his beloved, but once again relents, admitting that order must prevail in the cosmos. All of this takes place in a soliloquy, Rojas' magnificent after-

[25] GREEN, «The Artistic Originality of the *Celestina*», *Hispanic Review,* 33 (1965), 15-31, at p. 26. See also my «María Rosa Lida de Malkiel on the *Celestina*», *Hispania,* 50 (1967), 174-81, at pp. 179-80, and the references there.

thought, one of the great moments of the post-1499 portions of *Celestina*. We overtake Calisto out of character, and yet the scene is believable. What moved Rojas to give us this strange moment? Was this pure poetic invention, a spontaneous piece of character development, or was there some more complicated motive? It is impossible to say. What is certain is that Donatus, writing on Terence, notes with approval certain breaches of decorum he permits himself. It is not only a question of courtesans who are admirable against expectations, or generally of the character who as a whole does not conform to type. Our commentator calls attention to temporary lapses. Thraso in the *Eunuchus* is self-important and stupid, but in one of his lines he is less foolish than usual. The detail does not escape Donatus, who remarks that a comic figure that was uniformly witless would give no pleasure (on *Eunuchus*, 446). In the same play Parmeno remarks on how love has changed his master. Donatus comments that Phaedria's silliness can be attributed to his infatuation (on *Eunuchus*, 226). Later in the play Chaerea says to Parmeno that he must have Pamphila by fair means or foul. This outrageous remark is excused by Donatus as out of character: «non hoc personae attribuendum est sed affectui» (*Eunuchus*, 320); it is not Chaerea speaking, but love itself. None of the actual situations in Terence's play is anything like the one I have been speaking of in *Celestina*, but the bits of commentary do lay down a statute which covers it. Calisto's soliloquy is remarkable on several counts. The issue is not a simple one, but I believe it safe to say that the long speech in its setting is the only bit of the action of the play that is plainly indecorous; it is in any case one of the very few. It stands out on just this account. It is striking that a text as prestigious as Donatus' should sanction such a move of Rojas so perfectly and completely. The commentator in our three cases offers two motives for the poet's deviation, in one case his concern for his audience, and in the other two the character's strong emotion. Either reason fits the soliloquy. In one instance we say that Calisto is more interesting, if he is not uniformly distracted. The other instance poses a small difficulty in that he is already in the bonds of passion, but on the other hand the reason for his change is indeed effective. When he has satisfied his strong desire for the first time, his passion slackens temporarily and he is for a moment able to be concerned about things other than love.

The exception proves the rule. If indeed Rojas had Donatus or something like him in mind when he conceived the soliloquy in Act XIV, it would seem fair to conclude that problems of decorum were a serious concern of his. Melibea also is a thoroughly decorous character, though in her case we are dealing with two motives, love and honor; on Calisto's side there obviously is only love. Perhaps the personality of Melibea as conceived by Rojas is the ultimate and severest test of a *Celestina* reading

55

which stresses decorum and types. Melibea is a round character, if there ever was one. This vital young woman in time reveals many sides of herself. She is resolute before Celestina's intervention and resolute after, resolute in rejecting Calisto's suit, and later resolute as his mistress, despising marriage, proud of her status. The development in between is of course extraordinary. In her first interview with Celestina she begins as if unaware of the old woman's purpose, continues by protesting too much, and ends dropping the hint to Lucrecia and to us that appearances aside, she is not indifferent to Calisto. The second interview is the masterpiece of *vorrei-e-non-vorrei*. It is useless to try to paraphrase this magnificent scene: its issue is of course her frank confession of love. Does not this full and rich development exclude out of hand all thought of types? Not necessarily. Rojas' own text gives us a partial answer. In Act VI Celestina is trying to convince Calisto that his suit is not hopeless. In a devastating speech she assures him that the only difference between women of high estate and prostitutes is that the former acquiesce only after a long delay. Her language is strong, and it reveals a good deal about the substance of Celestina herself. It oversimplifies the concept of honor and says nothing about fidelity. All that is little enough. If we recall Melibea's severity in the first scene and her broad sensuality in the two nights of love, the truth of Celestina's remarks is largely vindicated. There are simply very few motives in Melibea's story and development that fall outside the old woman's generality. Let us be realistic. When we say that Melibea is lifelike, a full and well-rounded character, we are thinking largely of two things, first the contrast between her initial chastity and her later abandonment to passion, and second, the art and subtlety with which the transition is presented. The first state is entirely generic: the chaste Melibea has little that distinguishes her beyond her vigor and resolve. In her last state, what is most significant is her contrast with Calisto. Both are mad and imprudent lovers, but Calisto's vitality is low —Lida de Malkiel's very wise observation (*Originalidad*, pp. 354-58)— while Melibea never loses her vigor and forthrightness. This is simply a case of Terentian twinning, the feature so often noted by ancient and modern commentators: Terence loves to give us pairs of contrasting characters within one species, a passive young lover along with a more resolute one, an indulgent old man and a severe one.[26] But *Celestina's* two lovers are entirely of a piece: «adolecen del mismo mal.» Here is Melibea in love, as presented by Lucrecia. Her speech is nothing more than a rosary of commonplaces about the lover's unhappy state:

> Áme fuertemente dolido tu perdición. Cuanto más tú me querías encobrir
> y celar el fuego que te quemava, tanto más sus llamas se manifestavan en

---

[26] DUCKWORTH, pp. 184-90. For twinning as noted in older commentators, see ROBBINS, pp. 91 ff. On twinning in *Celestina*, see LIDA DE MALKIEL, pp. 265-80.

la color de tu cara, en el poco sossiego del coraçón, en el meneo de tus miembros, en el comer sin gana, en el no dormir. Assí que contino se te caían, como de entre las manos, señales muy claras de pena... Pero, pues ya no tiene tu merced otro medio sino *morir* o *amar,* mucha razón es que se escoja por mejor aquello que en sí lo es. (X.49-51, emphasis mine)

About Celestina I have little to say, for the moment at least. She is daunting, for one thing: she is inexhaustible. And in any case, she been written about so extensively: her prehistory, in particular, is a well-tilled garden. We may deal with her under four headings. First, she conforms to type. The species is not Terentian, but largely medieval and post-medieval: one must recall the *anus* in *Pamphilus de amore,* Urraca in the *Libro de buen amor,* and Callimacha in Johannes de Vallata's *Poliodorus.* Second, she is remarkable for her malice: in this sense she resembles certain characters in the humanistic plays. She deceives the servants, lies to them, although she does neither to her client. She is destructive. Pármeno's situation is comfortable: he has every practical reason to be faithful to Calisto and maintain solid order in his master's house. But Celestina does everything to put him at odds with Calisto, and in effect to reduce the boy to his former state. She also works hard against Areúsa's interest. The latter is well maintained by her friend, and would have been wise to remain faithful. But under pressure from Celestina she gives herself to Pármeno with nothing whatever to gain (as far as the text tells us). Celestina is old. The old, according to Horace, are concerned with wealth and gain, and so is she: this is a trait she shares, curiously, with another aged person in the play, Pleberio. The two are assuredly an unlikely pair: they are poles apart, in estate, in morals, in interests. But I do not believe that their common concern for wealth and gain is an accident. Age and wealth is a literary theme, and is embodied in the character of both.[27] Celestina is of low station, and she is therefore base. I shall have more to say on this subject presently.

Pármeno is also base, and this aspect of his personality will also have to wait to be examined. He has other qualities which we must look at first. It is easy to sentimentalize Pármeno. Decline and fall, native decency corrupted, a fine young man come to grief, all these are themes that his story might suggest. We may also find him interesting as a character who develops: he has a history, as many of his fellows in *Celestina* do not. Those who wish to stress the modernity of the *Tragicomedia* and its affinities to works recognizably realistic might tend to emphasize just this dynamism in Pármeno. But perhaps there is less drama in his life than meets the eye. Let us start at the beginning. Is Pármeno really vir-

[27] ROBBINS (pp. 73-77) gathers in one place references to the traits of the old in literature, in Aristotle and Horace as well as in Donatus and Renaissance commentators on Terence.

tuous? We must ask this question without prejudice. He does counsel Calisto wisely. In his first dialogue with Celestina he appears to express genuine concern for his master's well-being. But there is one factor that might count against this supposed goodness. This is his advantage of the moment: the boy has much to gain by being very faithful to Calisto. Pármeno is no fool: both authors make this quite clear. Born in very poor circumstances, he is now a member of a splendid household: he has security and quite a bit more. His good sense along with his unhappy memories give him every motive to be concerned for Calisto and to wish him well. His loyalty, as long as it lasts, is indeed hardly vicious, but neither can we call it ethereal, wholly self-effacing, or free of all selfishness.

In the long run, as I suppose, the question of Pármeno's virtue is undecidable: neither author chose to give us evidence enough to go on; the issue of interest or disinterest is left hanging in the balance. One further factor, however, might also count against the boy's moral excellence: Pármeno is changeable.

Change, as one might say, is Pármeno's pathology. It is in any event his distinguishing mark. His nearest competitor in the play might be Areúsa, with her complicated love-life: she abandons one lover and takes two others within days. Aside from hers, Pármeno's case is unique in *Celestina*. We see him first in the rôle of Celestina's biographer: he has known her since childhood, and as she stands at Calisto's door, the young servant tells him clearly and at length exactly who she is. Moments later he makes an aside: Calisto has offered her payment, and the boy, shocked, laments bitterly his master's involvement with the old woman. Then the great miracle happens. Celestina fires the whole arsenal of her dialectic at the youngster, and although he knows her malice very well he is soft, and confesses that her arguments and promises have puzzled his will: he is distressed by her anger, and would genuinely like to believe her. After their talk is over, Sempronio asks in effect whose side he is on, and Pármeno cautiously answers that he is on his (and hers). But this new bond is forgotten by the next time he comes on stage: Pármeno by this moment is plainly counselling Calisto to have nothing to do with Celestina. Angry words follow: Calisto accuses him of being a bad servant and of not taking his interests to heart. Pármeno, infuriated by his master's unreasonable and unfair response, declares to himself that his good will towards Calisto is at an end. This affirmation is the end of chapter one, so to speak, the first phase of the young servant's career. Exactly how long has Pármeno's virtue and loyalty lasted? The sequence of time in *Celestina* is never wholly clear, but the period in this case has got to be short. The issue of Pármeno's good faith does not even arise until he realizes that Calisto is to be the old woman's client. The conversation with Celestina which makes such an impression on the boy takes place within her first visit to Calisto. This latter ends as she is sent home in Sempronio's company and the unhappy lover is left alone with Pármeno, and it is at this moment that the unpleasant exchange between them takes place, at the end of which Pármeno resolves to break faith with his master. Pármeno's loyalty is asserted, tried, apparently broken, restored and then ended for good, all over a period slightly longer than that of Celestina's first visit, that is to say, minutes. This reflection should put to rest all notions about Pármeno's spectacular fall from virtue. His loyalty is to all appearances a simple whim of the moment.

Pármeno's changeableness does not end here. We see him next in Act VI, in the scene in which Celestina has returned to Calisto's house with Melibea's girdle. The young servant's attitude is curious. Assurances aside, he has not yet made his peace with Sempronio. And on the other hand, his wrath at Celestina is renewed. His anger is unreasonable: she is ever her old self, but in this case he truly misjudges her. He recognizes all her wheedling, but also accuses her of deceiving Calisto, and this latter allegation is entirely unjust. Celestina is indeed pulling out all the stops, doing everything to win Calisto's good will and to get him to favor her with gifts, but in her account of the visit to Melibea she is absolutely and literally truthful. Pármeno simply cannot accept this possibility. We could remark here that the other myth about the boy's personality, his supposed shrewdness and perceptiveness, stumbles on this very episode. At this point in the story we are treated to still another change. In the course of an ensuing conversation Pármeno asks Celestina to give him Areúsa. As we know, the scene ends at the young woman's house with the couple in bed: the boy is experiencing love for the first time. The next morning he returns to Calisto's house, euphoric, offering peace and good will to Sempronio, once for all. From that point on Pármeno's intentions do not change: he is to be ever of one mind with his fellow servant.

Such is Pármeno's variegated and wrinkled career. One could say that in the conception of his character a fine effect is produced by a very simple means. Pármeno gives an impression of depth and truth, but a great part of this fullness is brought about by an instrument no more complicated than making him change many times. At the head of this section of our study I promised to try to reconcile the way the tragicomedy's characters are presented with old notions of decorum, and with the idea that the individual becomes significant when associated with a species. I believe that such a reconciliation can be worked in this case. Pármeno is young. That propensity to change which so thoroughly characterizes the young servant is first and foremost a sign of his youth. Aristotle in the *Rhetoric* says that the young are «changeable and fickle

in their desires» (1389a) and Horace in the *Ars poetica* declares them
«quick to abandon a fancy», «amata relinquere pernix» (165). I see no
reason why these prestigious texts could not have had a part in the
formation of Pármeno's dramatic personality. We recall that in the
prefatory matter in Donatus age, the conformity of a character to the
ways of his age, was one of the «personarum leges», norms of decorum.
If Rojas had any respect for considerations of this kind, as he most
probably did, Horace and Aristotle would have been obvious places for
him to turn to for topics about youth. We could, of course, scuttle all
such notions and chalk up the invention of Pármeno's personality to
Rojas' own wit, working apart from literary conventions. One factor
favors the other view, however. Pármeno fits perfectly Forster's definition of a «flat» character.[29] This, by the way, may seem an unreasonable
judgment, but it is not so. He is lifelike, one might say, because he is
changeable: that gives him a density, an anomalous quality that has the
note of truth. But changeableness is itself the formula: a flat character
is one that is typified by a single trait. And as I have insisted, mutability,
the lack of constancy and resolve is precisely what typifies Pármeno. I
return to my own notion of global character. In Pármeno's case, as in that
of other *Celestina* characters, the list of general and global personal traits
is very small: I shall return to this theme. And the very shortness of
these lists seems to imply a simple and schematic characterology, which
in turn may reflect topoi, some sort of common matter: general ideas
about personality of the sort presented in Aristotle and Horace. Pármeno's many moods therefore need not be a simple caprice on the part of
the authors.

The last section of our study is not about a single character, but
about a group. It is also about a single motive. Our first authority is
Reginald Heber, who, as some of us recall, wrote of «Ceylon's [alterna-
tively, Java's] isle» that «every prospect pleases, and only man is vile».[30]
Rojas and his predecessor, as I believe, would have restricted vileness
even more, not to simply man, but to only some men and women. Américo Castro many years ago wished us to see a two-tiered world in *Celestina*: there was the idealized sphere of the lovers, and the picaresque set
inhabited by Celestina, the prostitutes and the servants.[31] I was informed
—by Stephen Gilman, in conversation— that Castro eventually abandoned this view. Perhaps his retreat was not wholly justified. Castro's
terms are to my mind wholly inaccurate, but to abandon all distinction
between great and small in *Celestina* is, as I think, to miss a great deal

---

[29] E. M. FORSTER, *Aspects of the Novel* (London: Edward Arnold; New York:
Harcourt Brace, 1927), pp. 103-04.
[30] *The Church Service Book*, G. Edward Stubbs, ed. (London: Novello, 1906),
p. 466.
[31] *El pensamiento de Cervantes*, p. 24.

of its point. Robert Burton, in the early seventeenth century, has a description of lovers' malady which restricts the disease to the well-born: the coarse temperaments of the base are more than enough to protect them from such ills.[32] I am not aware that earlier writers ever made quite this distinction. Within the system it seems logical enough: would a heavy-skinned laborer in the fields or a miner ever be subject to such exquisite torture as the lover undergoes? It is striking that although sex is everywhere in *Celestina,* the only characters to suffer from *amor hereos* strictly speaking are Calisto and Melibea, both of high estate. We have no evidence that Sempronio ever suffered such pangs on Elicia's account. Areúsa, as we have noted, entertains a third lover within a period of perhaps less than three days: her light-heartedness is scarcely compatible with the melodrama the medical texts envision.

Vileness, baseness takes many forms. Coarseness of sensibility is certainly base. Elicia goes into mourning, even though she means to continue plying her trade. But as her profits fall off, she sets her mourning aside. All this within days of Sempronio's death. Both prostitutes hate Melibea. Elicia appears to be jealous of her, as though Sempronio felt some attraction to her. His calling her «gentil» is enough to send the prostitute into a rage which she will not abandon as long as they all are at table. Both young women declare that Melibea is plain, even repulsive. This is an important point. Where does the truth lie, with them, who think her ugly, or with Calisto and the majority, who think her fair? The question is quite unanswerable: we have no third witness. But it is also irrelevant. Sempronio, who calls her «gentil», lives in the company of the well-born and knows something of their world: this means that he has some understanding of the phenomenon we could broadly call courtly love. To be sure, he may take no part in that whole practice, but he knows its language and its patterns. In courtly love there simply is no such thing as an ugly lady: Melibea can be nothing but «gentil». It is of course significant that one of Sempronio's lines early in the discussion is about the high birth of both the lovers, and their suitability to each other. The coarseness of sensibility of the prostitutes lies in the fact that they cannot grasp anything to do with gentility, Melibea's beauty, Calisto's love. They reduce everything to their own level: Elicia alludes to her own beauty.

It would be a mistake, as I think, to read this scene with democratic eyes, or worse, to charge the women's obtuseness to social causes. The whole sequence at Celestina's house is a display of crude emotions; un-

---

[32] *The Anatomy of Melancholy,* part III, sect. 4, memb. I, sub. I. This text is quoted in JOHN LIVINGSTON LOWES, «The Loveres Maladye of *Hereos*», *Modern Philology,* 11 (1913-14), 539; the whole article (pp. 491-546) is, of course, the classic treatment of its subject.

reasonable anger, bitter envy, and the reaction to the supposed *gentileza* of Melibea is a part of the crudeness. Areúsa and Elicia are base, and there's the whole problem. We have, after all, a parallel situation of a low-born character who is insensible to things noble and gentle. She is the infinitely more intelligent and perceptive Celestina, as she is trying to convince Calisto that Melibea will yield to him in time. This is the speech I have alluded to before. Be of good heart, she says to the young man; the only difference between gentlewomen and prostitutes is that the latter accede to men's wishes out of hand, whereas the former must delay. This is a devastating speech: it is brilliant, because it conveys two messages at once. On one hand Celestina reveals a solid knowledge of the gentle world. She knows that honor for the well-born is a serious issue. What is still more striking, she understands courtly love, and the drama that attends a woman's accession, if it is delayed. But on the other hand, her utterance reveals much about Celestina herself and her own estate. The speech is insulting. It so reduces and simplifies the theme of honor as to bring all gentle and noble ladies down to the level of prostitutes: the only difference is in the delay. The old woman's words also express her own perspective on love. First a prostitute herself and then a procuress, she sees love only and exclusively from the point of view of physical pleasure. It is useless to moralize, and award the judgment to Celestina, saying that indeed the two lovers are lustful. As I have already pointed out, the old woman has left out an important ingredient in high love, that is, fidelity. The text tells us many times that love among the base is promiscuous, but can we seriously suppose that our two noble lovers play their parts in their melodrama so that each can abandon the other out of hand and seek other partners? Reducing Melibea to the level of a prostitute is strictly speaking unjust. Celestina is base, and her speech tells us so in an eloquent way.

Rojas is in no way exalting love among the noble: we must be very clear about this. High love for him is pathology, as it was for many before him and many after. But on the other hand, nobility in this view is by no means a matter of indifference. It is among other things an innate quality, or set of qualities. One nobly born is naturally disposed towards certain habits, towards certain actions and passions. The fine temper of such a person, unhappily for him, makes him particularly susceptible to the sort of excruciating and obsessive passion described in *Celestina.* Its presence in some person is in itself hardly a good thing, but destructive as it may be, it is a sign of a certain excellence otherwise. And by the same token, inability to undergo such a passion is in the short term fortunate, but is fundamentally a sign of a coarse and ignoble temper, incapable of anything good.

Cowardice and interestedness are also base. Celestina is hardly a coward, and at times her behavior is straight and fair, witness generally her dealings with Calisto. But both her courage and her limited justice are traceable to her self-interest. She is a rational person, and knows that in her admittedly evil trade she cannot withdraw in the face of danger, or lie to a client. Pármeno at one moment seems to have taken Calisto's interest to heart. But we have seen how brief that moment was, and how fragile that bit of generosity. Noble qualities never appear in him again. Both he and Sempronio are cowardly. We recall the latter's mutability speech in Act III. It is long, and is his disproportionate reaction to a casual remark of Celestina about the dangers servants undergo when their masters are in love. Pármeno's cowardice does not surface until late in the play: the issue simply does not arise. But on the last night of his life, as he and Sempronio are standing near the door of Melibea's house, it is he, the younger servant, who first cries danger. We recall the moment. Calisto asks him to see if Melibea has kept the appointment. He refuses, saying that when she saw a stranger at her door, the young woman would conclude that the lovers' secret was out, or worse, that Calisto had abandoned her. In his very next speech Pármeno tells his fellow servant the real reasons. It is unnecessary to repeat the list: every item spells unreasonable caution. The remainder of their dialogue, as we know, is taken up completely by their expressions of fear, their mutual comfort in vice, and their declaration that they will flee before the least danger. They consummate their foulness in the following scene: their rage with self and their shame impels them to kill Celestina; Gilman's most eloquent page is the one dedicated to this last unutterable piece of cowardice (*Art,* pp. 102-03).

The all-wise Rojas has devised yet one other manifestation of baseness in his play. This strain involves a rhetorical pattern which I believe is his invention: it is something quite new. Consder the following speech uttered by Elicia, lamenting Celestina's death, to Areúsa:

> ¡O Celestina sabia, onrada y autorizada, cuántas faltas me encobrías con tu buen saber! Tú travajabas, yo holgava; tú salías fuera, yo estava encerrada; tú rota, yo vestida; tú entravas contino como abeja por casa, yo destrüía, que otra cosa no sabía hazer. ¡O bien y gozo mundano, que mientra eres posseído eres menospreciado, y jamás te consientes conocer hasta que te perdemos. (XV.17-18)

Taken out of context is there anything in this speech that would be inapplicable to the president of Catholic Action, or to an official of Ladies' Aid? Do these words tell us anything about the speaker? Might she not be one engaged in laboring among the poor of Calcutta? Let us understand: Elicia's words are not uttered humorously. We must distinguish. The narrator in the *Libro de buen amor* thinks kind thoughts about the departed Urraca: she must be among the martyrs in Heaven, such were the trials of her life on earth. Elicia's speech is nothing like this: it is not humorous to the fictional speaker and it is not humorous to the audience. The lament is indecorous: it is indecorous with respect to the fictional speaker and with respect to its subject-matter. It is, however, profoundly decorous in one sense. It is the utterance, accurately conceived and constructed, of a speaker who has, precisely, no sense of decorum: the fictional character Elicia is represented as not having any idea whatsoever of what words are appropriate to her, and to the matter she is treating. We recall Cicero's discussion of decorum in the *De officiis* (I 96-98). Decorum is of two kinds, moral and poetic. Moral decorum is the fitness of a person's actions to his nature. It is, obviously, a moral quality: it is an individual's resolve to behave in accordance with his humanity, generally, and with his virtues and vices, and with his life circumstances, in particular. Poetic decorum is the configuration of traits, actions and speeches the poet chooses and invents to be in accord with his general conception of his dramatic character. In reference to Elicia's speech we may say that it is hardly fitting to its speaker or to her subject matter: in other words, she reveals herself as morally indecorous. But on the other hand, the poet is presenting a base character whose taste and sensibility are so coarse that she cannot find the proper register for her speech and her theme: he therefore is observing poetic decorum.

Lack of moral decorum is very nearly the distinctive mark of Rojas' characters generally. The dull-witted old stable boy Sosia, bumbling, unimaginative, has a mode of speech that is entirely ludicrous. The odd pace and rhythm of his bookish rhetoric is one of the triumphs of idiom in the *Celestina*. The contrast between the solemnity of his diction and the deep simplicity of his thoughts is everywhere remarkable. But the great showcase of indecorum, the most memorable and remarkable, is Areúsa in the dinner scene at Celestina's house. Areúsa has turned philosopher. We are in the midst of the bitter dispute about the *gentileza* of Melibea: both prostitutes have vilified her, Areúsa last. Sempronio rejoins that the consensus of the town is that Melibea is beautiful. Areúsa answers:

> Ninguna cosa es más lexos de la verdad que la vulgar opinión. Nunca alegre bivirás, si por voluntad de muchos te riges. Porque estas son conclusiones verdaderas: que cualquier cosa que el vulgo piensa, es vanidad; lo que habla, falsedad; lo que reprueva es bondad; lo que aprueva, maldad. Y pues este es su más cierto uso y costumbre, no juzgues la bondad y hermosura de Melibea, por esso, ser la que afirmas. (IX.25)

Sempronio argues to the contrary, and answering Areúsa's «I can't understand what he sees in her», says that both lovers are of excellent lineage, and that her attraction for him is thus nothing out of the ordinary. She answers:

Rüín sea quien por rüín se tiene. Las obras hazen linage, que al fin todos somos hijos de Adán y Eva. Procure de ser cada uno bueno por sí y no vaya a buscar en la nobleza de sus passados la virtud. (IX.27)

The temptation is there to read these lines with Jeffersonian eyes, as though Areúsa were affirming the inborn dignity of the human species through the mouth of its humblest and most despised member. There are three arguments against this view. First, it is hard to believe that Rojas could have had anything of the sort in mind, or that his first readers could have gotten anything similar out of the speech. Second, in the piece about popular opinion Areúsa has used an elephant gun to shoot a rabbit. To air a formidable Senecan commonplace about moral self-sufficiency to attack a young woman's reputation for beauty, tells us more about the speaker's bitterness and envy than about the girl's appearance. As for her second answer we must remark that there is nothing virtuous about Areúsa. The third argument against a democratic reading of these lines is what I take the history of the influence of just this text to be. More of this later: I return to the second. Areúsa does not embody human dignity. She is a prostitute; not a great-hearted prostitute, or a fundamentally noble one, let us note. She begins as a kept woman faithful to a single lover. But as we have noted, we see her at one point bound by love, not by interest, to a worthless man, this before she even knows that Pármeno is dead. She attempts murder. Calisto, however witless, surely does not deserve to die. God forgive us all; Areúsa is nasty and she is crude. For this woman to invoke Stoical topics as she does, without humor and without irony, is simply a mark of her Johnsonian «stark insensibility», and there's an end on it.

Early in this section of the study I said, roughly, that I meant to vindicate the idea that *Celestina* is strongly bound to its past. In one sense our reflections about indecorous characters satisfy this program. It combines two notions any fair humanist would surely be familiar with, decorum as a moral virtue, and decorum as a rhetorical and poetic virtue. But on the other hand the very peculiar combination of the two is, as I believe, utterly and entirely new: here we are assuredly breaking faith. Its profound novelty may escape us precisely because the pattern nowadays is so familiar: what novelist's trick is more commonly applied than making a character reveal himself as he uses a register that does not suit him, or as he says things that are wildly inappropriate to him? But can we think of an instance earlier than *Celestina*? Let us be exact: we are not at this point speaking of dramatic irony, the situation in which a character might speak inappropriately, because he is ignorant of his real circumstances. The issue here is character. I do not think it extravagant to say that the important pattern I speak of is an invention of Fernando de Rojas. I return to my third argument against a democratic interpretation of Areúsa's short speeches. How did certain men of letters a few generations after Rojas read these passages? The answer to this question is a whole literary genre, and its name is picaresque.[33] Picaresque is, incidentally, the likeliest model and inspiration for later writers who chose to invent indecorous characters. Indecorum is the essence of the picaresque hero. It defines him: he would not be what he is without it. Lazarillo thinks himself a man of honor even though he willingly shares his wife with the archpriest. He believes his father is in Heaven, because he suffered persecution for justice's sake. Pablos lists the surnames in his mother's family: every one of them is typically *converso,* but for him the array of saints' names is proof that she was descended from the twelve Apostles. He never eats meat pie without saying a prayer for the faithful departed. Guzmán's discourse is exceptional among picaresque narratives: he of course is entirely self-aware, and knows very well what he is saying. But with this dramatic exception the picaresque narrator speaks out of insensibility. His baseness and ill-mixed temper keeps him from understanding fully everything he himself is saying. I cannot believe that this extraordinary literary invention is anything but an echo of *Celestina.* Or, to be more exact, the fact that picaresque has the profile and personality it has suggests strongly to me that its authors must have been forcibly struck by certain moments in the career of Elicia, Areúsa, Sosia and indeed Celestina. They could, of course, have made a serious error in judgment: their reading of the *Tragicomedia* could have been inaccurate. But why need we make this assumption? Cultural history is not an easy subject, and nothing is more constant in life than change itself. But in broad terms we can assert that between the time of the publication of *Celestina* and the date of the composition of *Lazarillo* the great *umwelt,* the order of accepted values, the shape of humanism and literary culture, had not greatly changed. The anonymous author of the later text is indeed a fair witness. Lazarillo's mode of being is certainly a short path to our understanding of Areúsa.

[33] Cfr. *La vida de Lazarillo de Tormes y de sus fortunas y adversidades,* ed. Alberto Blecua, Clásicos Castalia, 58 (Madrid: Castalia, 1974), Introduction, especially pp. 26-27 and 39-40.

III

RHETORIC

As I have stated before, this whole book is concerned first and foremost with the common and not the particular. My attention is focused not primarily on the things that are unique in *Celestina,* but on those that it shares, or might share. The structures which especially interest me are the ones which in my judgment could have been in the minds of the authors and their contemporaries, intended by the former, generally perceivable by the latter. Practically speaking this last condition tends to involve us in paradox, appearance versus reality; the common strain, genuine enough, is something we are not nowadays programmed to see. Thus in my remarks about genre I was obliged to confess that few contemporary readers would spontaneously say that *Celestina* resembles a Roman comedy, even though the authors and others of their time most probably conceived the species comedy broadly enough so as to include our famous text. What seems anomalous to us may have been to the eyes of another day natural, or indeed essential. As our discussion passes from genre to our next subject, rhetoric, much the same paradox emerges as before: the basic engineering of *Celestina,* perfectly recognizable to its first readers, is scarcely visible now, and even to call attention to it in latter days seems an impertinence, an intrusion of the scholar into the happy world of the reader and his book. For the two authors and for thousands of their contemporaries rhetoric was very nearly the only systematically taught writing technique available, and yet the whole system is so alien to us, its distinctions and contrasts are often so far removed from anything we might call the practice of literature that we will not believe that its norms were actually in force in the work of our eminent pair. Modern readers are confronted by a well-woven and significant text which they more or less understand and whose excellence they do not doubt, and it may prove very difficult to persuade them that there is in it a whole network of formal patterns and relationships which they have left out of account.

But the rhetoric is there, nevertheless, in obvious ways and in unobvious. Its presence in *Celestina* is easy to verify: many of the remarks that follow have no other purpose than to show how pervasive it is in our text. Perhaps some of the resistance modern readers might feel towards this sort of investigation may be lessened if we compare such an enterprise to a study of meter in a poetic corpus. Should we regard it as a striking coincidence that every one of the lines in Garcilaso's sonnets has eleven syllables, or that the stresses there follow certain patterns? Alternatively, must we attribute all this uniformity to some wild creative initiative of the poet? Obviously not. But the catch is that knowledge about hendecasyllabics is consecrated, whereas comparable knowledge about, shall we say, *exergasia* is not. Rhetoric is boring, some might think: it codifies the trivial. What is *chronographia*? The description of a time (Winter, or the month of May). What is *topographia*? The description of a place. Or consider this: «Sominex is effective. It works for me.» This is rhetorical, for the appeal to experience is a figure, *martyria.* Could we not conceivably describe an unpleasant winter, or the city of Muncie, Indiana or recommend an insomnia remedy without using rhetoric? This question and its fatal answer would seem to close the subject. And yet it does not. First of all, there is the plain question of fact. The two authors, like most of their literary contemporaries, really did know the figures and other rhetorical devices they could choose from, just as Garcilaso knew what meters were available to him. And in any case, rhetoric is by no means so idle nor empty as certain bits of it make it seem. To codify the sort of things I have described not only makes them fully present to the student and practitioner, and renders their use conscious to them; much more important, the items themselves become members of a repertory or paradigm, a complex of choices not invented by the author. *Chronographia,* for example, becomes one of a large body of figures of description, and the whole range of these patterns puts a large complex of possibilities into the orator's hand instantaneously. The consequences of this coding for the modern reader of old texts are obvious. A poet's facility at description may have more to do with his mastery of the code than with his observation of the world, and the modern assessment of his inventiveness or originality will thus be greatly displaced; the poet's initiatives will seem to be different in kind and different with respect to the area where it is effective.

The literary historian's attention to rhetoric forces many such displacements on him: this is a serious difficulty generally. Let us take a concrete example. Perhaps a majority of readers nowadays regard fiction as a privileged literary mode, one of two or three at the most (lyric poetry might be another). The novel, fiction par excellence, sets a sort of standard. What happens when one such normal reader is confronted by the *Libro de buen amor*? He will immediately dive into the narrator's account of his amorous adventures, skipping over the doctrinal parts, the discussions of Nature, astrology and the like. If our reader is also a critic, he will declare that the genius of Juan Ruiz lies precisely in his storytelling, in the liveliness of his presentation, and of the embarrassing plausibility of the material he narrates. If our commentator takes any note at all of the doctrinal material, he may dismiss it as a curiosity, or again, he may ironize it to death, attributing it to the whimsical temper of the poet. Lovers of literature live and die by such convictions. They will therefore not take kindly to an interpretation which picks up the other option. Start with the lines on astrology and Nature, one would say, and let us see where that leads us. Could it not be that most of the narratives are simply examples meant to bear out the truths set forth in the doctrinal passages? The poet redolent with learning and letters invokes Aristotle as his *auctor,* as he declares that fundamentally humans and brutes alike crave food and sex. Is it any accident, then, that the *Libro* tells its story as it does? After forty days of austerity, as the poet has it, the two emperors who come to take over the world are Don Carnal and Don Amor. And more generally is it not striking that one important episode of the poem is devoted to the gratification of hunger, just as most of the rest is given over to the narrator's amorous adventures?

These are, of course, the thoughts of a rhetorician. General propositions are brought into the text to highlight the significance of particulars, or conversely. Story becomes *exemplum,* bearing out the truth of the thesis. For the reader of the *Libro de buen amor* such notions force on him a displacement of his attention, perhaps to his displeasure; his gaze will have to shift from what seemed most significant to what least. We may generalize. Rhetoric, unclassical in Barthes' sense, at odds with nineteenth and twentieth-century notions of composition, will force on us many such shifts of attention. That is one of the difficulties we run into as we turn to the question of rhetoric in *Celestina.* Even though this study is not really meant to be literary criticism, my propositions will invite the same displacement of attention I have spoken of. This shift will of course lead to some readings that may seem counterintuitive: the speech we thought mostly affective may now prove argumentative, or the ironical passage may now make sense taken literally. The difficulty is unavoidable: philology was not invented to make people comfortable.

These remarks stand as a warning. Exegesis is not the aim of this discussion, as I keep repeating, but it is nevertheless practically impossible to practise positivism in literary studies without at some point its affecting the ways in which texts are read. Without further comment, then, I launch into a scrutiny of the *Tragicomedia*'s rhetoric, one figure at a time, starting at the beginning.

1. ARGUMENTATION

Rhetorical argument can be found in the very first speech of *Celestina*:

CALISTO: En esto veo, Melibea, la grandeza de Dios.
MELIBEA: ¿En qué, Calisto?
CALISTO: En dar poder a natura que de tan perfeta hermosura te dotasse, y hazer a mí, inmérito, tanta merced que verte alcançasse, y en tan conveniente lugar, que mi secreto dolor manifestarte pudiesse. Sin duda incomparablemente es mayor tal galardón que el servicio, sacrificio, devoción y obras pías, que por este lugar alcançar yo tengo a Dios ofrecido. ¿Quién vido en esta vida cuerpo glorificado de ningún ombre, como agora el mío? Por cierto los gloriosos santos, que se deleitan en la visión divina, no gozan más que yo agora en el acatamiento tuyo. Mas, ¡o triste! que en esto deferimos: que ellos puramente se glorifican sin temor de caer de tal bienaventurança, y yo, misto, me alegro con recelo del esquivo tormento que tu ausencia me á de causar. (I.1-4)

Calisto here uses three figures. First he supports a general proposition. «En esto veo la grandeza de Dios» with a group of proofs, Melibea as Nature's masterpiece, God's graciousness in allowing him to see her, and so on: this amounts to a species of *diallage*. Next he compares his good fortune at being in her presence with the lot of the blessed in heaven, a *comparatio,* affirming the greatness of something by comparing it to a thing generally believed great. Finally, he makes a distinction: the blessed need not fear that their happiness will end, but he must, since he will not always be with her. This is, of course, *dissimilitudo,* both figure and topic.[1]

Stephen Gilman speaks volumes of truth when he states that argument and sentiment are two of the fundamental modalities of the dialogue in *Celestina,* yet his prime example of sentiment, Areúsa's long declaration of independence in Act IX (*The Art,* pp. 24-25), is in fact belligerently argumentative and rhetorical. The version of 1499 has the speech begin with a general proposition about the wretchedness of those who serve ladies: «Assí goze de mí, que es verdad; que estas que sirven a señoras ni gozan deleite ni conocen los dulces premios de amor» (IX.45). It continues with a particular instance to the contrary, Areúsa herself, who is not in service: «Por esto me bivo sobre mí, desde que me sé conocer. Que jamás me precié de llamar de otrie sino mía» (IX.47). These lines give us a virtual syllogism: those who serve ladies are unhappy, I wished to be happy, therefore I am my own person, and no

---

[1] *Diallage* in Quintilian, *Institutio Oratoria,* IX.2:103; *comparatio,* VIII.4:11; *argumentum a dissimilibus,* V.10:73.

one's else. The longer version has Areúsa argue with still more force: she adduces examples to confirm her major premise:[2]

> Nunca tratan con parientes, con iguales a quien puedan hablar tú por tú, con quien digan: «¿qué cenaste? ¿estás preñada? ¿cuántas gallinas crías? ¡llévame a merendar a tu casa! ¡muéstrame tu enamorado! ¿cuánto a que no te vido? ¿cómo te va con él? ¿quién son tus vezinas?» y otras cosas de igualdad semejantes. (IX.45-46)

This inductive proof is, in the bargain, seasoned with a good bit of *dialogismos,* the figure in which the speaker assumes the voice of another person (Quintilian, IX.2:31).

Celestina cannot abstain from argument. The issue can be anything at all. Should Sempronio see Celestina home or not? That is the question. It is indeed subject of a very formal debate. Calisto asks his servant to accompany the old woman and to tell her of his master's passion. Calisto urges three reasons for the latter: «que de su diligencia pende mi salud, de su tardança mi pena, de su olvido mi desesperança» (II.7). *Diallage* once again. He concludes by saying that his desperate love makes him inarticulate, but that Sempronio, unaffected, can plead his cause: «Tú, como ombre libre de tal passión, hablarla as a rienda suelta» (II.8). Love impedes speech, Calisto is in love, Sempronio not, therefore Sempronio should speak, not Calisto. The servant's answer is also rhetorical. It is a *deliberatio* or *dubitatio* (Quintilian, IX.2:19). On one hand, says Sempronio, I should obey, but on the other I fear leaving you alone in your desperate state. He multiplies examples of signs of this state: «sospirando, gemiendo, mal trobando, holgando con lo escuro» (II.9). You will lose your mind or even die, if someone is not on hand to cheer you: once again, an implied syllogism. The speech concludes with a cluster of examples of the companion's proposed good turns: «te allegue plazeres, diga donaires, tanga canciones alegres», etc. (II.10). Calisto answers appealing to a generality; weeping relieves pain: «¿no sabes que alivia la pena llorar la causa?» (II.11); Sempronio responds with another *sententia*: «Lee más adelante; buelve la hoja. Hallarás que dizen que fiar en lo temporal y buscar materia de tristeza, que es igual género de locura» (II.12). The servant argues not only by assimilating the particular instance to a general rule, but adduces an authority (the unspecified *auctor* of the text one reads, «lee») to support the premise. The appeal to authority is of course, a standard procedure in rhetoric, an inartificial proof, requiring no art on the part of the speaker when he uses it.[3]

---

[2] Cfr. CICERO on *ratiocinatio, De inventione,* I.57 ff.
[3] Quintilian, V.2:2. HENRY PEACHAM calls the appeal to authority a figure, apomnemonysis, *The Garden of Eloquence,* facsimile of the 1593 edition with portions of the 1577, ed. W. G. Crane (Gainesville, FL: Scolar's Facsimiles and Reprints, 1954), p. 87.

Rhetoric is by modern convention fulsome speech, and it is unnecessary to stress that not everything in *Celestina* is fulsome. There are moments that are in this modern sense anti-rhetorical. One such is found in the otherwise heavily oratorical and dialectical interchange between Pármeno and Celestina in Act I. Pármeno has just framed a formidable argument from potency and act:

> en los bienes mejor es el acto que la potencia, y en los males mejor la potencia que el acto. Assí que mejor es ser sano que poderlo ser, y mejor es poder ser doliente que ser enfermo por acto. Y por tanto, es mejor tener la potencia, en el mal, que el acto. (I.134)

Celestina punctures his balloon: «¡O malvado! ¡Cómo que no se te entiende!» (I, 135). Rhetoric mocked, as we might say. But this mocking is itself a rhetorical procedure, in time identified as a figure, *antirrhesis*, rejecting an opponent's argument by mockery.[4] Rhetoric is many things. Carmelo Samonà perceives the following as within *Celestina*'s non-rhetorical register:

> SEMPRONIO: Espantado me tienes. Mucho puede el continuo trabajo; una continua gotera horaca una piedra.
> PÁRMENO: Verás qué tan continuo; que ayer lo pensé, ya la tengo por mía.
> SEMPRONIO: ¡La vieja anda por aí!
> PÁRMENO: ¿En qué lo vees?
> SEMPRONIO: En que ella me avía dicho que te quería mucho y que te la haría aver. (VIII.22-23)[5]

But this text includes a *sententia*: «Mucho puede», with its implied assimilation of the particular to the common, an *exemplum*: «una continua gotera», and an *aetiologia*, Sempronio's account of how he knows that Celestina was at work. The most perfunctory turns of dialogue can become dialectical. In Act IV Celestina hesitates to speak, but Melibea urges her on: «Di, madre, todas tus necessidades, que si yo las pudiere remediar, de muy buen grado lo haré, por el passado conocimiento y vezindad, que pone obligación a los buenos» (IV.48). Still another syllogism: neighborhood obliges, I was once a neighbor, therefore I am obliged. Finally, we may cite a feature that in isolation, at least, seems hardly literary. Lucrecia lists the signs that show that Melibea is in love: «en la color de tu cara, en el poco sossiego del coraçón, en el meneo de tus miembros, en el comer sin gana, en el no dormir» (X.49). The speech as a whole is indeed by ordinary standards oratorical, but the point here is that the plain citing of instances, the simple reference to the facts of

---

[4] Quintilian (IV.1:38) makes deprecating an opponent's argument one of the procedures in refutation. IX.2:106 applies the term *antirrhesis* to refutation globally, but PEACHAM limits it to mockery (pp. 88-89).
[5] *Aspetti del retoricismo nella «Celestina»* (Roma: Studi di letteratura spagnola, Facoltà di magisterio dell'Università di Roma, 1953), p. 179.

Melibea's life, is a rhetorical procedure. Signs constitute another species of inartificial proof, of a piece with evidence generally, witnesses, speakers under oath, proofs in general that may be simply advanced, and require no art on the side of the orator.[6]

It would be impossible in this brief study to list by genera and species all the figures, topics of invention, or forms of argument in *Celestina*. More than that, it is unnecessary: any student wealthy enough to own a Quintilian or a Lausberg can point out figures as well as I.[7] Rhetorical argument in *Celestina* is in any case pervasive: the proportion of the text that disputes, argues, convinces according to the old patterns is very large. We may generalize in two areas. First, the long speeches in *Celestina,* so typical of the work, are the eminent case. There are, of course, passages in the play that plainly and patently are oratorical, and it needs to be stressed that they are such in the full sense: they are convincing just as they are copious. Their very bulk is made up in part of figures and other devices that argue and advance reasons. The accumulation of proofs to support a single proposition, the inductive proof, in which a number of special cases sustains a broader truth, the airing of the whole and its parts, the genus and its species, the subject and its adjuncts, the long procession of generalities and *sententiae,* sometimes passing over the same ground, sometimes linked in one or another kind of logical pattern, the generality followed by particular instances, and above all the mixed form, the *expolitio,* in which a single theme is confirmed in many ways, by example, by comparison, by contrast, by other generalities: these are the devices we see used again and again in the long speeches in the great drama, in the first act as in the rest. The speeches so structured appear in a variety of settings. Often they stand alone, surrounded by more informal dialogue, but occasionally they are piled up sandwich-wise, when pairs of characters exchange them in virtual *controversiae.* As we know well, some of the great scenes of *Celestina* are laid out in just this way.

Second, there is the *sententia. Celestina* is sententious, like Shakespeare and the Elizabethans, much more so than its supposed models, more than Terence, more than the elegiac comedies, more than most of the humanistic plays. To the extent that it is sententious it is also argumentative. Our aesthetic prejudices may stand between us and the *Tragicomedia.* The myriad *fontecicas de filosofía* in our play do more than give it gravity or fullness of diction. As we recall, the proposition with the universal subject is treated in rhetoric under two headings, as a *locus*

---

[6] Quintilian, V.9:1. In paragraphs 1-3 he distinguishes between signs which are inartificial and those which are artificial. Cicero in the *Topics* XII deals with signs under the heading of adjuncts.

[7] HEINRICH LAUSBERG, *Manual de retórica literaria: fundamentos de una ciencia de la literatura,* trans. José Pérez Riesco, 3 vols. (Madrid: Gredos, 1966-69).

communis, part of *inventio,* a general statement meant to give weight to arguments about particulars,[8] and the *sententia* proper, a figure belonging to *elocutio,* aphorism, well-turned phrase, one more grace in the text of the completed speech. The *sententiae* in *Celestina,* identifiably just that, also retain their *locus communis* personality as the examples I have cited very clearly show. If we want further proof, we need only look at one example among many, Sempronio's great speech at the beginning of Act II, a long train of *sententiae* about liberality and honor, meant (cynically) to convince Calisto that his gift to Celestina was well-made. So many others. Behind every *sententia* lurks a syllogism.

I conclude the descriptive portion of this study with two brief observations. I remark first that *Celestina* must in a sense be its own document: we must read it on its own terms. As I have pointed out, the work argues almost continuously: it argues when the issue is important and when, to us, at least, it seems less than important. Rhetoric is well into the foreground of the *Tragicomedia.* To fail to see it there, or, still worse, to overinterpret it, whenever it seems absurd or impertinent to us, is to forego the possibility of a very privileged reading of the drama. Our second point is that the scope of rhetoric in *Celestina* is local. We may gratefully make our own Gilman's proposition that the art of Rojas is dialogic, that its scope and end is to give words and arguments to different voices, voices which address one another. More modestly, we could say that the work argues one issue at a time. The dialectic of Pármeno and the figures which realize it are in a literal and primary sense his: they are designed to support his case of the moment, his interests of the moment. Sempronio's *sententiae* on liberality and honor are first and foremost meant to convince Calisto that he has acted wisely. The individual speeches and the rhetoric that in most cases makes them up are the elementary building-blocks of *Celestina*: our readings of the drama should be grounded in this basic proposition.

What I said about the sententiousness of *Celestina* could be repeated about its rhetoric generally. It may be viewed as prophetic: it must be viewed as unusual. None of the older dramatic texts with affinities to the *Tragicomedia* are in our sense as rhetorical, not Plautus or Terence, not the elegiacs, not the Latin comedies of the fifteenth century. I readily admit that I am speaking of very different species, and indeed of different degrees of rhetoricality, but my point stands. What set of circumstances, then, witnessed the birth of our strange and singular Spanish drama? To what factors can its very special profile be attributed? There are, as I believe, three. The first is the obvious one, rhetoric itself. Not the meager medieval rhetoric, *dictamen* plus decorative figures, as in San Pedro, but the full Quintilianesque art, total in its ambition, including

[8] CICERO, *De inventione,* II.48.

argument and all its works. Of the first author's training we know nothing, but Rojas' surely was solid and broad. In his day at Salamanca, roughly that of Lucio Marineo Siculo and Antonio de Nebrija, the *artes dicendi* generally taught must have been of the generous sort, and we cannot imagine our second author seriously deprived.[9] The second factor complements the first. It is the two authors' reading of Terence. Rojas' years of study and *a fortiori* those of his predecessor were such as to deny them access to any but one or two of the very earliest Renaissance commentaries on the six comedies. This is a pity, because such access might have explained a great deal: the commentaries are with few exceptions full of rhetorical comment. But the commentary certainly available to both, that of Donatus, is by no means devoid of rhetorical lore. Donatus' text, or one like it, could well have been the one to lay down the proposition to our authors that comedy can be rhetorical. Detail after detail in the six plays of Terence is assimilated by Donatus to the laws of oratory. Thais' long (and interrupted) speech to Phaedria in the first act of the *Eunuchus* is analyzed as a formal oration, disposed with a *principium, narratio, confirmatio, reprehensio* and *conclusio*. Davus' soliloquy in the first act of *Andria* is described as a «breuis et comica deliberatio». A great variety of figures is pointed out, including many which bear directly on dialectic, *epagoge* (induction), *peristasis, syllogismos, metalepsis*. The first scene of the third act of *Hecyra* is «quasi quaedam deliberatiua continens suasionis dissuasionisque partes»: the details of the argument are discussed in their proper places. The comment on *Adelphoe* 478 is among other things a general account of artificial and inartificial proofs. On a virtual syllogism of the sort I have spoken of in *Celestina, Hecyra* 59, Donatus says «huiusmodi sententias rhetores *dianóias* uocant». *Andria* 372 is called an enthymeme. Most dazzling of all, perhaps, is Donatus on *Hecyra* 589. The verse runs: «illius stultitia victa ex urbe tu rus habitatum migres»; the commentary has «*illius* a persona; *stultitia* a causa; ... *ex urbe* a loco; *tu* a persona: *habitatum* a facto... uide quam oratorie omnia congesserit: a personis, a causis, a locis, a factis».

That Donatus' commentary on Terence should contain rhetorical lore is, of course, in no way remarkable: the strong alliance between oratory and poetry is ancient and perennial. I must emphasize, however, that the rhetoric our commentator finds in the plays is nearly all local, in the sense I have given the word to date. Most of the devices Donatus points out have to do with the design or detail of the utterances of individual speakers, or at most, of pairs of speakers in virtual debate. Quite un-

---

9 NEBRIJA's own rhetoric is an anthology, witness its title *Artis rhetoricae compendiosa coaptatio ex Aristotile, Cicerone & Quintiliano...* (Compluti: Arnaldo Guillermo de Brocar, 1515).

typical are discussions of the rhetoric of the ensemble, so to speak, of each play, *qua* play, as a whole or even in part. By contrast, this is precisely the approach of many Terentian commentators of the Renaissance. Melancthon and Willichius consider *Andria* an example of deliberative oratory and Cordatus viewed the same play as a sustained *controversia* on the issue of whether or not a young man should marry. Willichius turned each scene of the plays into a little oration, each with its *exordium, narratio,* etc.[10] This contrast between the approaches of Donatus and his successors, local, with an eye to dialogue, on one hand, global, concerned with dramatic discourse, on the other, is to my mind highly significant, for reasons I have already made clear.

The issue at hand is the manner and mode of the *Celestina*'s authors' reading of Terence. It matters very little whether or not we consider Terence oratorical. It is enough that with their training they did. Terence was a school text, and if students from their first encounter with his plays were taught to see this detail as an enthymeme, that as an induction, a third as an *exemplum,* and still another as a set of arguments drawn from the topics of invention, they might well have ended considering those works very argumentative indeed. The observations of the sort Donatus makes would have obliged our two authors to read Terence —and indeed Plautus, and the humanist comics— in a very special way. It is not outrageous to view *Celestina* itself as a kind of reading of Terence. The Renaissance interpreters, who are still more rhetorical than Donatus, are in some cases Rojas' contemporaries, and their respective products, Rojas' and theirs, in a genuine sense parallel phenomena. I could add that the very rhetorical theater of a later day was the product, significantly enough, of men who knew Terence commentaries as I suppose Rojas and his predecessor may have, and that the broad similarity of design of one and another may grow out of this common background.

A third, perhaps less important, factor in the formation of the rhetorical *Celestina* is the influence of the humanistic comedy. We should distinguish: the global influence of Latin plays of the Quattrocento on the *Tragicomedia* is incalculable; the latter is, in fact, language apart, one of their number. But their influence as precisely rhetorical drama is more limited. In one respect the Latin plays are unlike *Celestina*. The impulses behind their formation are twofold, rhetorical, assuredly, but also imitative. It is silly to reduce these works to a formula, but it is obvious that the humanist authors went to lengths to imitate ancient models in detail, Plautus, probably, more than Terence. Much of the body of these texts

---

[10] MARVIN T. HERRICK, *Comic Theory in the Sixteenth Century* (Urbana: Univ. of Iillinois Press, 1964), p. 14 for *Andria* as deliberative in Melancthon and Willichius, pp. 6 ff. for Willichius on the structure of each scene, and p. 179 for Cordatus.

is made up of dialogue, turns of phrase, situations which are plainly supposed to look and sound like analogous things in Roman comedy. This leaves less room for argument and rhetoric, less typical of the Romans, and in fact the fifteenth-century plays are less rhetorical than *Celestina*. There are in them, nevertheless, passages which are very Celestinesque. The *Philogenia* of Ugolino Pisano in its earlier pages makes its protagonists argue with each other in a way that should be very familiar to us. A page or so of *Poliodorus* could sink into *Celestina* without leaving a trace.[11] There is, in a word, an occasional tendency in these plays to argue which does not look especially Terentian or Plautan, and which might well have set the example for our two Spaniards.[12].

Quintilian is all a poet needs, said Ben Jonson, more or less. True with respect to Rojas and his predecessor, if we add Terence and his commentator, and perhaps the example of the Italians. It should be clear by now that the rhetoric I refer to is not that of Samonà in his study of the *Celestina*, a repertory of expressive devices. It is not exactly even the rhetoric of Spitzer, who saw in the authors' use of the art a key to the meaning and sense of the whole play (pp. 8-9). Is my rhetoric, then, reductive? Is my conception of argument and persuasion in *Celestina* such as to diminish seriously its scope, its richness, its complexity? In one sense I can shamelessly answer yes. We need only say the obvious: *Celestina* is inexhaustible, and there is no magic key to its comprehension. But on the other hand it is a great mistake to undervalue rhetoric itself, its great power and scope, and much of what we admire in *Celestina* is well within its range. There is the character and activity of Celestina herself, her power over others, Pármeno, Areúsa, Melibea, Calisto, the rest. This power is realized by the authors, and can be understood by us, largely through rhetoric: «Celestina is Spain's finest orator», as Gilman says.[13] The interview with Pármeno in the first act, one of the work's great scenes by any standards, is a long and crowded procession of *sententiae*, enthymemes, *exempla*, inductions and more. What more brilliant conception than the first encounter of the go-between with Melibea? The older woman shows her perverse wisdom by dwelling endlessly on her own age, on the passing of her beauty, on the passing of pleasure, all to bring home to Melibea the truth that her own youth and beauty will pass.

---

[11] JOHANNES DE VALLATA, *Poliodorus: Comedia humanística desconocida*, ed. José María Casas Homs (Madrid: CSIC, 1953), p. 207, has a piece of dialogue, virtually a debate, between the Celestina figure and the heroine which is full of *sententiae*.

[12] LEO SPITZER in «A New Book on the *Celestina*», *Hispanic Review*, 25 (1957), 1-25, at p. 9, proposes the tragedies of Seneca as a model for *Celestina* as rhetorical drama. I believe, however, that my proposal, Terence-cum-commentary, brings us closer to the detail of the Spanish drama.

[13] *The Spain of Fernando de Rojas: The Intellectual and Social Landscape of «La Celestina»* (Princeton: Univ. Press, 1972), p. 314.

A magnificent instance of Quintilian's *ratiocinatio* (VIII.4.15-20) in which a discourse is designed to let the hearer draw for himself the conclusions intended. Broader structural aspects of *Celestina* are also plainly rhetorical. Surely, one of the things we admire most about the work, an aspect that gives it much of its richness and power of suggestion, is its polycentricity, its *polyphony* in Bakhtin's sense (I am not suggesting that *Celestina* is necessarily polyphonic absolutely, though it may be). I return to the notion of the locality of rhetoric in the play. The art is designed to argue cases, and quite aside from the causes the whole work may be defending, it is clear that each of the characters, moment by moment, defends his own, whatever that may be. We may very properly speak of the dialogic or perhaps controversial art of Rojas and his predecessor: the drama of our text resides in great part in the succession and interchange of speeches, each with its own logic, a logic literally and primarily meant to address the issues raised within other speeches. Finally, there is irony. Irony in *Celestina* also lies within the possibilities of rhetoric. Preceptists since Aristotle have spoken of the need for the orator to be a just man, and have insisted that his art serve just causes. But in the essence of things rhetoric is indifferent to the character of the speaker or of his aims. It is also indifferent to his degree of knowledge. The orator may make a malicious speech, he may also make a foolish speech, ignorant as he may be of his real situation. Both sorts of speakers inhabit *Celestina*. Irony is generated by the malicious speech, because the audience recognizes his lies and knows the degree to which the fictional listener is deceived. Irony is generated by the ignorant speech obviously and essentially, in that the audience knows what the speaker does not. Not only are both of these structural features, polyphony and irony, possibilities implicit in rhetoric proper: rhetorical drama, of the sort readers of the commentators are led to see in Terence, contains both patterns. The rhetoric, real or imagined, of the six comedies is exploited by the several characters in each and serves a variety of ends. And all of the plays are peopled by deceitful orators as well as ignorant ones.

* * *

Celestina is a humanistic comedy, so it has been said. It belongs to this species: it may be longer than other examples, it may be better or more ambitious, but the only formal trait that separates it from its fellows is its language, not Latin but Castilian. But as I have tried to show earlier in this essay, the Humanistic Comedy should perhaps not be regarded as a separate genre at all: it is likely that in the mind of its authors its representative texts were comedies, simply. In other words the norms that governed the composition of the Roman plays of Plautus and Terence were broad enough to sanction the practice of the writers

of a later day. In our eyes, of course, in those of a twentieth-century
reader, the gap is fairly wide between a Terence and an Ugolino da Pisa,
between the old plays and the relatively new, but what should concern
us in this set of differences is not primarily the plain anomaly, but rather
the question of how exactly the humanists of the fifteenth century read
the ancient comedy. This question is not new to us: I have considered
it at length earlier in this study. But the subject is not closed. One thing
is certain: the fifteenth-century comics thought that the Roman comedy
was rhetorical. This will become obvious as my study progresses. As I
have said before, it scarcely matters whether or not we consider Plautus
and Terence rhetorical: it is simply significant that the humanist authors
did. Their bias is surely not an accident. It may be traced to the importance generally of rhetoric in the fifteenth century, or, as I have suggested regarding *Celestina,* to the commentaries on Terence which they
read, which present the plays as rhetorical. Now, the prominence of argument and rhetoric in *Celestina* plainly has to do with the fact that it is
on some level one in kind with the *Cauteraria, Paulus, Philogenia* and
the rest: all of these texts are rhetorical for more or less the same
reasons. With all this in mind, it may be interesting to see in what ways
the *Tragicomedia* is or is not distinctive with respect to the humanistic
plays. I have already suggested that it is more rhetorical than its fellows.
The time has come to specify, to point out the exact extent to which it
stands apart.

Let us begin by looking at one of the great scenes in *Celestina,* the
passage in which the old bawd brings Calisto the news of her first interview with Melibea. This splendid moment is, as we recall, a chaotic
exchange made up of two conversations, between the old woman and her
client, and between the two servants. The scene is replete with figures.
In Celestina's first speech, in which she highlights the risks of her mission,
she caps a string of rhetorical questions with a *comparatio,* «Mi vida
diera por menor precio que agora daría este manto raído y viejo» (VI.1):
the figure dramatizes the danger. The allusion to the mantle is also an
instance of *emphasis* or *ratiocinatio,* indirection:[14] she calls attention to
its shabby state so Calisto will give her a new one. To Calisto's «o abrevia
tu razón o toma esta espada y mátame» (VI.3), she answers «¡Espada mala
mate a tus enemigos y a quien mal te quiere!» (VI.4) and then announces
her good news. The line quoted expresses a universal, «swords are meant
to kill enemies», and so forms the major of a virtual syllogism; the minor
is, of course, «you are fortunate and not your own enemy», and the conclusion, «I should not kill you with your sword». *Emphasis,* be it noted,
is plainly Celestina's favorite medium —witness her remarkable and

---

[14] *Comparatio:* Quintilian, VIII.4:9-14; *ratiocinatio:* VIII.4:15-21. Donatus
in the commentary calls this figure *emphasis.*

extensive use of the figure in her interviews with Melibea— and in the present scene she once again combines it with *comparatio* in a second allusion to her clothes: «antes me recibirá a mí con esta saya rota, que a otra con seda y brocado» (VI.4). To Pármeno's sour reaction Sempronio answers that she has a right to beg: his proverb-*exemplum* «el abad de do canta, de allí viste» (VI.5) expresses a generality, «everyone has a right to earn a living in his own way». Pármeno's answer is yet another *comparatio*: for one simple errand she wants to be paid more than she has earned in fifty years. Even Sempronio's warning, «Calla, ombre desesperado, que te matará Calisto si te oye» (VI.3) could pass as a figure, *cataplexis*, a scheme drawn from the topic *consequents* (Quintilian, IX.2:103). All of these figures occur in a space of some thirty-five lines. We could continue at pleasure. This density of rhetorical devices in this very passage is above all a paradox. The scene is in no obvious sense oratorical: the rapid exchange would in its nature seem to foreclose the possibility of eloquence and formal argument. The naïve reader, and perhaps many less naïve, would surely identify it as one of the least rhetorical of the play, one in which the dialogue seems closest to ordinary conversation. I should cautiously suggest that this invasion of rhetoric and argument into informal dialogue is one of the distinctive triumphs of the *Tragicomedia*. The mixture is in any case not peculiar to this passage: it can be found in many more. Perhaps nothing is more symptomatic of this invasion than the presence of complicated bits of argument in some of the most trivial and peripheral turns of the discourse. In their first interview Melibea is about to dismiss Celestina when the latter makes it clear she has more to say. Melibea urges her to speak: «Di, madre, todas tus necessidades, que si yo las pudiere remediar, de muy buen grado lo haré, por el passado conocimiento y vezindad, que pone obligación a los buenos» (VI.48). This again is a hidden syllogism: neighborhood and acquaintance oblige the good, I am a neighbor, and acquaintance, and am good, therefore I am obliged (to hear you out).

Rhetoric is thus present in passages that are in no obvious sense eloquent or fulsome. And yet the invasion of oratorical devices into the dramatic detail in *Celestina* does not end there. Formal debates, for example perfectly legitimate *controversiae*, turn up in *Celestina* on very mundane and unimportant subjects. Should Sempronio see Celestina home? We have already seen how thoroughly this lofty theme is argued on both sides. «Provide for the future», says the old woman on another occasion to a recalcitrant Elicia, who will not learn how to repair maidenheads. The old woman argues from the topic *consequents*, threatening a wretched old age, and adds an appropriate *sententia*: «la mocedad ociosa acarrea la vegez arrepentida y trabajosa» (VII.109). Elicia answers several lines later with her own set of generalities: «Mientra oy toviéremos de comer, no pensemos en mañana. Tan bien se muere el que mucho allega como el que pobremente bive, y el dotor como el pastor, y el papa como el sacristán, y el señor como el siervo» (VII.111-12). Both women argue from universals to particulars.

This strain, the invasion of formal rhetorical argument into the nooks and crannies of the dialogue where it seems least necessary, is indeed distinctively Celestinesque. We should remark that the passages where these rhetorical devices put in an appearance are not all the most contemptible. The spots where they are applied are successful, idiomatic, brilliant. Much of the color and savor, the variegated surface of *Celestina* can be traced to this near omnipresence of rhetoric. It is in any case one of the things that sets the great drama apart from the other humanistic plays. As I have pointed out, the Latin comedies of the fifteenth century are generally less rhetorical than the *Tragicomedia*: rhetoric in them seems to be occasional, reserved for special moments. The presence of rhetorical devices in ordinary conversational exchanges is rather less typical of the older plays. But, as we very well know, rhetoric in everyday life is not the only kind to be found in *Celestina*. There are, for example, debates, *controversiae*, on wholly serious subjects, central to the matter of the play. Should or should not Calisto be in love? This is, of course, the subject of several pages of dialogue between him and Sempronio. The servant advances authorities and examples to dissuade Calisto, and he for his part draws on the topics for the description of persons to convince Sempronio of Melibea's excellence. Should Pármeno keep faith with his master? He and Celestina have this one out in an impressive exchange replete with figures. Thus far the debate. There is another large feature, one I have alluded to, the most conspicuous pattern in *Celestina* generally, and the most obviously rhetorical, the long speech. As I have already stressed, these harangues argue —many of them, in any case: they are meant to convince, to persuade. Sempronio's parade of *sententiae* on liberality and honor is uttered to assure Calisto that the «cien monedas» were well bestowed, and his long string of examples of transience is designed to warn Celestina that Calisto's love may fade, and to urge her to strike while the iron is hot, and to play it safe (as he means to play it).

Two subspecies, therefore, two kinds of set pieces, the *controversia*, an old school exercise, and what we could broadly call the deliberative speech: both are prominent and important in *Celestina* and in fact both figure large in the Humanistic Comedy. With respect to the first genre we should have to specify. The trivial circumstance, as I have pointed out, is not generally a matter for debate in the older plays. When the controversies turn on particular questions, these tend to be themes fairly central to the plot. And curiously, there is a preference in the Latin comedies for debates on theses, on universal subjects, touching not determinate persons and things, but whole species. This particular feature is not very typical of *Celestina*, though it is by no means absent. Much of the rhetoric in the older plays falls into one of our two patterns, debate and persuasive speech, and, special cases aside, much in these Latin texts that looks and feels familiar to the readers of the *Tragicomedia* turns out to be in one or another of these two patterns. Consider the following debate scene in Vallata's *Poliodorus*. The young girl Clymestra feigns indifference towards the hero, but Callimacha, the Celestina-like character, urges her to yield to him. She argues from the universal nature of love: «res enim est innata nobis amor, et uetus non noua atque aliena; feras quoque que siluis habitant amoris tangit dulcedo» (pp. 207-08). She then accuses the girl of lack of feeling. The young woman in turn justifies this insensibility: «ne me delirare uoles ut id rei quod amorem appellas nobis una cum bestiis conueniat credam», etc. She adroitly turns the same universal-love argument against her opponent. A few lines further on she says «Non ille iustus est amor», and Callimacha answers:

> Ita tibi uidetur, Clymestra, quia amor quid sit non sentis. Ego, que aliquando sensi, testor nichil esse amore nobilius prestabiliusque adulescentie. Unde enim sumptuose uestes, unde ornamenta illa egregia nisi ab amore ipso orta sunt, que res iuuinilia magis exornat corpora? Illas omnes operas artesque sartorum, cerdonum, pellicariorum, aurifabrorum, nonne amor induxit? Quid plura? tu ne rem iniustam dicis quam dii probarunt? amarunt enim dii omnes, tu uero recusabis amare; sane non te putarem eiusmodi esse que quidem istis uerbis non mulier sane lapis quidem uisa es [15].

The speech is in good form. The old woman argues from experiencc, which is itself a figure, *martyria,* she produces an induction on the excellence of love, and continues with a *comparatio,* «the gods themselves love, but you do not deign to». Nothing here is strange to readers of the *Tragicomedia,* the arguments from generalities, the other figures. The accumulation, «unde enim sumptuose uestes», etc., might seem especially Celestinesque.

Everything gets debated in the humanistic comedy. Two characters in the *Cauteraria* argue about the virtues of wine. On the first page of the *Philogenia* of Ugolino da Pisa the hero's love itself is the issue (pp. 174ff.). The seduction scene in the same work is a splendid verbal set-to: should she or should she not? (pp. 183ff.). Vice and its consequences, temperance, the delights of love are subjects of talk in a later act (pp. 206-10). In the *Electoral Comedy* two candidates for an academic vacancy argue with each other about their respective merits (pp. 430ff.). In Vergerio's *Paulus* the wastrel student and his servant argue about whether the former should abandon his foolish ways and get back to work (pp. 54ff.). Some characters in the dialogue argue points by themselves. The wife in the *Cauteraria* argues that no amount of force can

---

[15] *Teatro goliardico dell'Umanesimo,* ed. Vito Pandolfi and Erminia Artese (Milano: Lerici, 1965), p. 478; page references henceforth to this text.

oblige a wife to remain faithful (p. 482). In Enea Silvio Piccolomini's *Chrysis* one speaker makes a case for the natural promiscuity of women. In these and in many similar passages much the same arsenal of rhetorical devices is drawn upon as in *Celestina*. Braco, the aged husband in the *Cauteraria,* uses a fine logic-chopping *climax* in pressing the virtues of wine: «Aiunt enim verum esse...bene bibentem bene dormire et bene dormientem non peccare, non peccantes autem in divino illo summo sempiternoque domicilio recipi manifestum esse» (p. 478). No character from the *Tragicomedia* could do better. Not a few utterances cited above are long and fulsome: some are inductions, strings of *exempla,* accumulations of some sort, others are mixed-media events with a variety of figures. *Philogenia,* the Latin play most like *Celestina,* resembles it in great part because of its processions of long speeches. The very first lines of Ugolino's great comedy, which starts with a notable *exemplum* and a *comparatio,* brings us close to home:

> Vere hoc possum dicere, mi Nicomi, in amore me perditum et miserum atque omnem etatem meam contrivisse, dum amori operam dedi: atque uno verbo expediam. Amavi frustra; dii boni, tanta ne duritia affectum quemquam ut amori non respondeat? Id profecto vitum ingratum virginum tanquam pernitiosum legibus Persarum gravissimis merito plecti solent. Et enim apud eos exploratissimum est quem alteri debere non suppuduerit, omnibus in rebus boni viri semper officium relinquere. Sed severius et durius, me Hercule, pena affici debent qui sinceri amoris, quam qui pecunie debitores effecti sunt, si nihil vereantur debitores naturae agnoscere quot debeant. (p. 174)

This piece of eloquence is not an isolated case. Perhaps nothing tells us better how conventional rhetoric and persuasion in the humanistic comedy were, or became, than some amusing lines in the late *Advocatus,* in which the art of discourse is actually alluded to. In a lurid triangle scene Racilia is attempting to justify her behavior to her husband. The lover remarks, «O quam pulchre utitur haec mulier insinuatione rhetorica!». The married couple continue arguing and the lover comments further, pointing out the commonplaces in their discourse, nothing less: «Quam similibus locis/Vtuntur hi, veluti parati convenerint/Huc ad recriminationem».[16]

The argumentative mode in *Celestina* is assuredly an inheritance from the humanistic comedy. Considering the character of the genre globally, it is hard to think of another model. Neither Terence nor Plautus will do. The rhetorical argument commentators found in Terence is at best virtual: the set pieces I have spoken of are surely not a part of the text itself. The elegiac comedies are certainly off the track; the Senecan model once proposed by Spitzer (p. 9) is by no means as close as the

---

[16] *«Veterator»* und *«Advocatus»,* ed. J. Bolte (Berlin: Max Hermann, 1902), pp. 117-18.

humanistic. If we were to ask where the argumentative strain in the fifteenth-century Latin plays came from, one might plausibly answer as I have when speaking of *Celestina*. I have traced the rhetoric in the Spanish play to the treatises themselves, to the influence of the humanistic plays, and perhaps most significantly of all to the Terence comentaries of Donatus, that is, to Terence seen through Donatus' eyes. There is no reason why this same sandwich, text plus commentary, should not have had a large part in the shaping of the general design of the older plays as a class. One could maintain that rhetoric and argument are native to drama as a whole, that one cannot put two characters on the stage without at some time making them argue, or having one try to persuade the other on some question or other. But the case of the humanistic comedies and that of *Celestina* are surely special: there is no nature so powerful as to compel their authors to ingraft into their texts codified and institutional forms of discourse, or to include argumentative material beyond the limits of verisimilitude. These features are distinctive: drama can do without them, and they are in these texts because their authors particularly wanted them to be there, and it seems plausible that the whole idea might be traceable to what must be one of the most powerful and well-known texts on rhetorical drama, Donatus' famous commentary.

Rhetoric in everyday life, as we have seen, is one element that separates *Celestina* from its immediate predecessors. Are there any others? I have already spoken of the invasion of rhetoric into the peripheral and prosaic dramatic situation, the prospect of Sempronio seeing Celestina home, Elicia's unwillingness to repair maidenheads, the old woman's second visit to Calisto. As I have said, passages like this are uncharacteristic of the older plays. A very few skate close: the scene I have alluded to from the *Advocatus* might do as an example, and there is an exchange in one of the plays of Frulovisi, a dialogue between a prostitute and her penniless lover, which is argumentative, but not quite a debate.[17] It is certainly true that in the Latin plays argument may break in at unlikely moments: this might seem to be the case particularly in some of the more broadly funny texts, like the *Cauteraria*. But as I have pointed out, the themes under discussion in such cases are not the minutiae of the situation, but universal topics, the virtues of wine, or the natural promiscuity of women, and this is not a characteristic register in *Celestina*. A much more important point of difference has to do with the quality we generally term dialogic (I retain the adjective, because I will not coin the abstract «dialogicity»). The dialogic and its opposite are plainly ideal types, and abstractions are treacherous. It is nevertheless

---

[57] *Titi Livii de Frulovisiis de Ferraria opera hactenus inedita,* ed. C. W. Previté-Orton (Cambridge: Univ. Press, 1932), pp. 71-73.

fairly safe to say that *Celestina* is more purely dialogic than its immediate dramatic precedessors. The history and background of this contrast is, as I think, interesting and is perhaps worth airing. We begin with Plautus and Terence. Plautus writes sparkling dialogue, but no single play taken globally comes anywhere near being dialogic. There are broad formal features that frustrate the dialogic quality, the famous Plautine prologue, for example, spoken by one of the characters addressing the audience, identifying himself, informing them in detail about the events they are to witness, and, in some cases, actually conveying a great part of the plot. In certain of the comedies this passage of information takes place well inside the body of the play. And beyond this, the audience in Plautus is always party to the goings on: numerous gags are aimed directly at them, bits of humor that have nothing whatever to do with the sustaining of verisimilitude. In no sense can the audience hold on to the illusion that it is overhearing real people, observing them unseen as they play out their careers. Terence is different: he departs from the usage of Plautus and perhaps from that of the whole New Comedy precisely in matters of this sort. His great innovation was precisely to put the audience in the position of simple observers. In the short run, at least, the viewer of these plays is not lured into complicity with the author and his creatures as happens in Plautus' plays. Not a little of what Gilman says about dialogue in *Celestina* is perfectly applicable to the six comedies. And I might well add here the observation made earlier that as presented by Donatus, Terence is more dialogic than ever: the rhetoric and argument pointed out in the commentary always belong to the individual speaker and his utterance and never primarily to the text of the play as a play. The humanistic comedies for their part are by no means alike: it is hard to generalize about them. Most of them seem more Plautine than Terentian, and that Plautine character includes some of the features I have mentioned. The *Cauteraria,* for example, has a prologue like that of the older Roman playwright, and in other respects too, some of the possibilities for dialogic drama seem to be shut off in them in a Plautine way. But quite as important, many of the humanistic plays steer away from dialogue in that the author makes his voice heard directly. He can hardly appear as a third-person narrator in drama, but he can play a rôle as judge, evaluating the actions of his characters. I have in mind, of course, one of the most familiar devices in comedy, the character «who speaks for the author», the *homme de bon sens,* the personage whose speeches express nothing other than reason and good judgment, in the light of whose sayings we evaluate everything and everyone else in the play. The predecessors of Molière are none other than Vergerio and Ugolino da Pisa. I am not, by the way, picking those names at random: the plays associated with each are classic instances of the pattern I haven spoken of. In one way or another, then, drama that is deeply dialogic is not very characteristic of the humanistic plays. The dialogic *Celestina,* therefore, represents a genuine initiative. Its patent solidarity with the fifteenth-century plays notwithstanding, it parts company with them in this respect, perhaps in direct imitation of Terence, perhaps following the guidance of Donatus, or perhaps independently.

2. STYLE

I keep protesting through the length of these studies that I am not concerned here primarily with what is unique in *Celestina.* This assertion may seem especially problematic, even absurd, when we talk about style. Style is a thumbprint—«Le style c'est l'homme même.» If style is not peculiar to a single work, it should certainly be distinctive to a single author. We may indeed speak of period style or generational style, but we tend to think of such things on the pattern of individual style, as though a group of writers had a collective personality, as though the spirit of a generation or of a time hovered over a sector of humanity like smog over Los Angeles. Some style studies in essence are concerned with the particular. I must confess that I am at a loss to think about style in this conventional sense with respect to the *Tragicomedia.* What is the style of *Celestina*? What is the style of Rojas, or of the first author? I find these questions unanswerable. Dramatic works in any case present a special difficulty in this sense, because they claim to record and represent many voices, not just one. One might conceive of a distinctive manner for Pármeno or Calisto, but hardly for the whole work, and even less for Rojas or his predecessor. But even here there are difficulties. As I have stated above, the moment we start to speak of what is unique in the *Celestina,* the things that are original, brilliant, genial, we are as likely as not concentrating on very local matters, the tone and manner of a Celestina of a particular moment, the savor and shape of Elicia's utterance at another. The manner and register change as each of these goes on to the next stage of her life. Not even characters have a style in *Celestina.*

We have been over this whole matter before. Our solution, of course, is to think of style in a completely different way, to reserve the term for something which is common, conventional and institutional, and on the other hand, to put the thumbprint, the unique manner, the distinctive profile, under a different heading, idiom, or ethos. Rhetoric after all, speaks of three styles, each appropriate for different kinds of discourse, and the problem I am concerned with is rhetorical. Although, indeed, one could think of *Celestina* as having more than one style, I shall not be much concerned with this plurality. My study will be selective: I shall fix my attention on a set of stylistic traits, not necessarily limited to one register, characteristics which are general and conspicuous in the text, a cluster of practices, however, which has a distinctive personality and history outside *Celestina*. Styles, like formal things generally, may have genealogies and histories just as other aspects of literature have, and my essay on style will by no means exclude such matters. Inevitably I shall have to double back and refer to topics I have already treated, but now serving new interests, and seeing old matter under a new species.

* * *

The authors of *Celestina* are prodigal with figures of contrast, broadly antitheses: there is scarcely a page of the *Tragicomedia* that does not have several of these. Here is a typical passage:

> Déxenme mis padres gozar dél, si ellos quieren gozar de mí. No piensen en estas vanidades ni en estos casamientos; que más vale ser buena amiga que mala casada. Déxenme gozar mi mocedad alegre, si quieren gozar su vegez cansada... (XVI.13-14)

There is more in the same mode. Antitheses are as frequent in the first act as in the others. The first author gives us: «el intento de tus palabras á seído: como de ingenio de tal ombre como tú, aver de salir para se perder en la virtud de tal muger como yo» (I.6); «Dile que cierre la boca, y comience abrir la bolsa» (I.122); «Paréceme que pensava que le ofrecía palabras por escusar galardón» (I.124). Rojas within a few pages offers us: «en el servicio del crïado está el galardón del señor» (II.13); «puede más contigo su voluntad que mi temor» (II.16); «Señor, más quiero que aïrado me repreendas, porque te do enojo, que arrepentido me condenes, porque no te di consejo» (II.20); «Valiera más solo, que mal acompañado» (II.23). Samonà in his study of rhetoric in *Celestina* calls attention to a form of antithesis, frequent in the work, which gives point and elegance to the *sententia*. He offers as an example: «Es menor yerro no condenar los malhechores que punir los innocentes» (p. 60). Other instances are legion. Frequent also are antitheses that contrast unequals, with an *a fortiori* sense, in the style of a *comparatio*: «esta puta vieja querría en un día por tres passos, desechar todo el pelo malo, cuanto cincuenta años no á podido medrar» (VI.6).

I stress the frequency with which figures of this type appear in our great text, because they are an index to a certain kind of taste, a taste, indeed, which is far from universal. Antithesis can be a sort of issue. John Dryden without using the term worries the subject to death. Chaucer, he says, follows Nature more closely than does Ovid. The practical sense of this judgment is that the Roman's language is «conceited» as the

English poet's is not. Narcissus in a passion unto death delivers an elegant paradox, «inopem me copia fecit»; Dryden takes no pleasure in the phrase.[18] Lines later, after a paraphrase of Chaucer he asks:

> What would Ovid have done on this occasion? He would certainly have made Arcite witty on his deathbed; he had complained he was further off from possession, by being so near, and a thousand such boyisms, which Chaucer rejected as below the dignity of the subject. They who think otherwise would, by the same reason, prefer Lucan and Ovid to Homer and Virgil, and Martial to all four of them.

We should note that Dryden here spoke more truly than he intended. The last sentence is supposed to be a *reductio ad absurdum*: people of taste do not relish conceit and wit, for if they did, they would rank Lucan over Homer, which is absurd. But, alas, whole generations of writers, not the least great either, effectively do rank Lucan over Homer and Virgil: the latter pair may have pride of place, but as effective models, Lucan and his like have no competition. Silver Latin generally, it cannot be repeated too often, has an importance for medieval and modern literature which has few rivals: by simple measurement the wake of a Seneca or a Lucan may prove to be wider than that of any more classic author. The humanism of *Celestina* is within this current, and in a sense its wealth of antithesis and related figures —its own tendency towards «conceit», in a word— tells us just that.

Celestina is rhetorical. This proposition can mean many things; at times it can express approval, but more often it expresses the opposite. Conventionally, rhetoric means bombast, wasted words: more narrowly, rhetoric tends to mean the saying of the same thing over and over again in a continuous stretch of discourse. Consider generally the use of «rhetoric» and «rhetorical» in a typical older manual of Latin literature. After Virgil and Horace, as we read, something goes wrong: Roman poetry and prose become rhetorical: «Rhetorical» in these contexts never seems to have a technical meaning: our attention is not directed especially to a figure or group of figures, not ordinarily to questions of *compositio* or to techniques of *amplificatio*. To the malicious reader what seems to be meant as much as anything is simply that Silver Latin is repetitious and that repetitiousness is bad. Menéndez y Pelayo in another setting plays on the same theme. Writing on *Celestina* he speaks not of rhetoric, but of the vices of its day. Of Rojas he says:

> en realidad amplifica y repite á cada momento: toda idea recibe en él cuatro, cinco ó más formas, que no siempre mejoran la primera. Esta super-

---

[18] *An Essay of Dramatic Poesy and Other Critical Writings,* ed. John L. Mahoney (Indianapolis: Bobbs Merrill, 1965), p. 103; all of my quotations from Dryden are from this page.

abundancia verbal se agrava considerablemente en la segunda forma de la tragicomedia, pero existía ya en la primitiva [19].

Where does all this leave us?

Menéndez y Pelayo's statements are accurate, of course. More than that, he has in these lines taken note of an essential and fundamental characteristic of his great text. Only the value judgment («agrava») is misleading, his sense that repetitiousness is an accidental vice in what is otherwise a work of genius. And for all of their wooliness on their subject, the textbooks of Latin literature are only stating the obvious when they speak of the rhetorical qualities of Ovid and Lucan. Writers of the Silver Age indeed love to say the same thing in several ways, specifying, dividing, accumulating examples or simply repeating in different words. The case of Seneca's tragedies is notable, particularly if we compare them with their models. Most frequently the Senecan play begins with a long speech, often spoken by the main character, in which the audience is brought up to date on the action to follow. Opening speeches of this sort of course occur also in Greek tragedies: they are often long, but, unlike those of Seneca, are progressive, passing from one subject to another at short intervals. But Seneca's prologuists stick to the point. Thus Oedipus declares that the Fates have prepared the worst, and continues listing manifestations of the plague at Thebes for more than forty lines. These lines follow another stretch of twenty-three on the trials of kingship. Dryden, once again, berates Ovid in a passage I alluded to: «Would any man who is ready to die for love, describe his passion like Narcissus? Would he think of *inopem me copia fecit,* and a dozen more of such expressions, poured on the neck of one another, and signifying all the same thing?» E. J. Kenney in a fine essay on the style of the *Metamorphoses* covers the same non-progressive style of discourse under the heading «theme and variations».[20] The passage occurs, significantly, in a section of his paper on rhetoric in Ovid, and it is a pleasure to note that there is nothing whatever woolly or untechnical in his discussion of that awesome subject. The most naïve reader of the *Metamorphoses,* needless to say, would have not the least difficulty finding many cases of «theme and variations» in his text. Finally, Gordon Williams takes us on a tour of the Silver Age, gathering up instances of «theme and variations» from all its great figures, once again highlighting and calling attention to something any student might come upon by himself.[21]

---

[19] *Orígenes de la novela* (Buenos Aires: GLEM, 1944), XIII, p. 192.
[20] «The Style of the *Metamorphoses*», in *Ovid,* ed. J. W. Binns (London: Routledge & Kegan Paul, 1973), pp. 116-53, at pp. 132-35.
[21] *Change and Decline* (Berkeley: Univ. of California Press, 1978), pp. 213-18. On repetititousness in Lucan as a Silver trait see also J. F. D'ALTON, *Roman Literary Theory and Criticism* (New York: Russell and Russell, 1962), p. 459.

«Theme and variations», the non-progressive bit of discourse, is another prominent feature of *Celestina* which binds it to Silver Latin. Again I must insist that I am not seeking to isolate some unique factor in the *Tragicomedia* which sets it apart in Spanish literature, or which tells us of the great independence of Rojas and his predecessor. The issue is taste. The two authors, both humanstically trained, were so formed as to respond to one kind of literary model and not another. And here, incidentally, we may safely speak of rhetoric and all its works. The non-progressive text is not a rhetorical figure simply, but the area it represents is well covered by a number of devices, *accumulatio, expolitio, divisio,* certain figures of description, certain sorts of proof, the accumulation of arguments to prove a point, the induction, the collection of instances to establish a general principle. *Celestina* is in this sense genuinely rhetorical, and so also is much of Silver Latin. It is precisely a certain sort of rhetoric that binds the two together.

Celestina, like the texts of the early Principate, is prodigal. Neither our tragicomedy nor Lucan's *Pharsalia* is remarkable for spareness, nor sobriety. Consider Sempronio's long speech on liberality at the beginning of the second act. This harangue is a long procession of general propositions, well-turned, not one of them original with Rojas, swelling up a speech by Sempronio whose sense is very simple —that Calisto did well to pay the old woman handsomely. As we know, general propositions, equally unoriginal, invade a large proportion of the speeches in our drama. In other words, *Celestina's* style is sententious: the text is full of *sententiae* —indeed it is lavish in its use of them. The «Carta del auctor a un su amigo» expresses admiration of the first author for no other reason: the latter is praised for the wealth of «fontecicas de filosofía» which decorate his fragment. «Gran filósofo era», said of the first author may be translated, «the first act is sententious». All this is well known. Equally well known is that prodigality in the use of *sententiae* is a mark of the style of Silver authors of the most diverse literary personalities. The sententiousness of the literature of the early Principate is pure topic: it is entirely fitting to say that sententiousness is one of the most characteristic traits of Silver Latin.[22] And, once again, rhetoric is a link with *Celestina,* for *sententia* is a figure of diction.

---

[22] WILLIAMS, pp. 207 ff. Anticipating my argument I refer also to S. BONNER, *Roman Declamation* (Liverpool: Univ. Press, 1949), in which he associates certain rhetorical devices in Silver authors with the influence of declamation. He speaks of *loci* in general on pp. 60 ff., in declamation on p. 79, of *sententiae* in Ovid on p. 144 and on p. 151, in Livy on p. 157, in Velleius Paterculus, p. 159, in Seneca's tragedies, pp. 160 ff., in his prose, p. 165. The multitude of *sententiae* in Silver Latin is one of its traits which he traces to the influence of declamation. J. F. D'Alton, see note 21, speaks of the effects public recitation had on poetry in the Silver Age, «the employment of devices already found effective in the schools of declamation— the forced conceit, the balanced antithesis, the flashing epigram»

Williams, once again, writing in general about the literature of the Silver Age has this to say: «Such expansiveness and the concomitant concentration on the single idea inevitably led to lack of interest in the strict coherence and movement of ideas and in the organization of the whole» (p. 215). He is describing here the course Silver authors charted between the poles of willful repetitiousness on one hand and *sententia* and epigram on the other, and is calling attention to the more or less informal disposition of longer portions of the text which was often the result. If we pass from Williams' large scale and global reference to the very small and local range represented by *Celestina,* we may find ourselves on similar ground. The same constraints are there, and the result is also much the same. I am thinking now not of the *Tragicomedia* as a whole, but of its basic unit, the single speech. Typically, almost universally, this stretch of text, if it is long enough, is simply a loosely organized collection of discrete bits, virtually interchangeable. Would the meaning be different, would we in any way lose the thread of thought, if we were to rearrange the pieces of Sempronio's speech on liberality or of his big «mutability» speech in Act III, or of any other of the long harangues in the play? The pattern is basic. I should add that in a sense it is hard to recognize. Although ordinary modern readers may find these *Celestina* speeches fulsome and excessive, their essential plan, the structure they share may go unnoticed because it is so common in expository prose nowadays. We have naturalized texts like these. For that very reason it is important to point out that this pattern, the sequence of bits whose order is not significant, is distinctive and is in no way normal: it is typical of Silver Latin and it is surely conspicuous in Rojas' *Celestina.*

It would be possible to continue this discussion at pleasure, pointing out one after another trait of style that unites *Celestina* to certain Imperial ancestors. I have certainly chosen the most basic of these characteristics.[23] We should note that each by itself, prominent in the *Tragicomedia,* is almost by convention recognized as an important trait in the literary style of our great period: it is no whim of mine that associates each with Silver Latin. And without claiming to explain fully this affinity of taste, certain facts make the parallel not seem accidental. Latin writings of the crucial period were certainly known to the authors of *Celestina.* Ovid and the younger Seneca figure large in the list of its

(p. 458). He speaks of the «profusion of epigrams» in the tragedies of Seneca (p. 460), of the moral maxims there (p. 461), and of epigram as «a favorite device in the prose of the Silver Age» (p. 212).

[23] Anticipating my own argument once again I cite Bonner's work on declamation (see note 22), pp. 68 ff. He lists and discusses the traits of style and the rhetorical figures of preference in declamatory texts. His list is longer than mine. Although his book is not primarily about belles-lettres, he does devote a chapter to the influence of declamation on other literary genres (Ch. 8, pp. 149-67), and so in speaking of Silver Latin he alludes to his own list of figures and devices.

sources; Lucan too is important and Persius is not absent.[24] Silver Latin influence also comes into the *Tragicomedia* indirectly. *Fiammetta,* notorious for its echoes in the Spanish work, depends heavily on Ovid's *Heroides* and the tragic Seneca. The Humanistic Comedy also, all-important for an understanding of our play, in many instances parts company with its models Terence and Plautus in the same way as *Celestina* does: these plays have in them not a little Silver Latin. Finally, there is rhetoric itself, a formative influence on all fronts. But here we must be very much on the alert. By involving rhetoric as a cause in common we run the risk of explaining not too little, but too much. Rhetoric recommends everything and nothing. It can account for fulsome utterances and also for plain; it can explain artful diction, but it can also explain diction which is apparently artless. The qualities Dryden hates are not in any decent sense more rhetorical than the ones he tolerates. One way or another we have to narrow our field. One mode of rhetoric, however, could indeed count as a decisive influence in both Silver Latin and in *Celestina.* This strain is present in the *Tragicomedia,* as I shall try to show, and at the same time we can count on conventional views to tell us that the same current is important in the prose and poetry of the early Principate.[25] I am thinking of the teaching and practice associated with declamation. It is this very important common influence that will concern us for the rest of the present study.

The declamation I am speaking of is a species of display oratory which became a form of public entertainment from the early years of the Empire on. In those years, as we can imagine, people would flock to hear well-known speakers debate on certain subjects, sometimes in mock court trials, at others advising heroes of history and legend pro and con on certain moral dilemmas —should Agamemnon sacrifice his daughter? Should Alexander cross the sea? Most of the speakers-performers were professionals who built reputations on just this kind of oratory. Our best witness to this whole curious institution is, as we know, Seneca the Elder, whose *Controversiae* and *Suasoriae* are a collection of excerpts from the speeches of the great declaimers of his day, along with comments and summaries of his own. These texts do not, alas, reproduce whole orations. For each debating topic proposed he gives us first a set of excerpts, purple patches, attributed each to one of his declaimers, and then, in paraphrase, the properly argumentative part of the speeches. The prefaces of many of the books have survived, and these are full of inva-

---

[24] F. CASTRO GUISASOLA, *Observaciones sobre las fuentes literarias de «La Celestina»,* Revista de Filología Española, anejo 5 (Madrid: Centro de Estudios Históricos, 1924), for Ovid, pp. 66 ff., Persius, pp. 79-80, Seneca the Younger, pp. 94 ff., Juvenal, p. 48, Lucan, p. 49.

[25] See note 23; Bonner's propositions about the influence of declamation are not unique.

luable information about the history and character of declamation. In the short run, at least, it is the collection of *excerpta,* which Seneca calls *sententiae,* which sheds the most light on our problem. They are intended to be models of style, and are indeed a showcase of all the qualities which interest us. They vary in length from a single short sentence to more than a page. Some of the longer stretches are simply groups of brief utterances, but others are plainly meant to be continuous. Dryden, if he knew this material, must have disliked every phrase: more obstinately witty or «conceited» language is hard to find, or, in the case of the long bits, more mountainously repetitive. We are in any case quite obviously on the turf of *Celestina. Sententiae* in our sense, which Seneca calls *loci communes* or simply *loci,* are everywhere. He speaks of them explicitly, in fact, and describes their function. The brief excerpts I spoke of are almost invariably marked by some kind of ingenuity, an artful paradox, or play on words, or a brilliant antithesis. Thus, on the question of whether Alexander should sail the seas Marullus contributes this: «Maria sequimur, terras cui tradimus? Orbem quem non novi quaero, quem vici relinquo.» On Agamemnon's decision on whether to sacrifice Iphigenia or not, Cornelius Hispanus offers: «Infestae sunt...tempestates et saeviunt maria, neque adhuc parricidium feci. Ista maria, si numine suo deus regeret, adulteris clauderentur.» Should the Persian trophies be taken down to satisfy Xerxes? Argentarius comments: «Non pudet vos? pluris trophaea vestra Xerses aestumat quam vos».[26] This turn, a comparison between unequals, is especially reminiscent of some of the antitheses of *Celestina,* of the sort I have pointed out. Figures of just this sort, antithesis and the rest, also invade the longer pieces in Seneca. In some cases they come at the end of a long tirade, and in others they pervade the whole excerpt. They are in any case omnipresent. «Theme and variations», finally, repetitious stretches of more or less interchangeable parts are also an important feature of Seneca's longer excerpts, as we shall see presently.

The influence of declamation on the literature of the Silver Age is beyond doubt: the naked eye, so to speak, perceives the kinship, and history confirms the intuition. And on the other hand, everything moves us to connect declamation somehow with *Celestina*: the parallels are obvious. Is a direct contact possible? Could the *controversiae* and *suasoriae* of Seneca actually figure in the list of the *Tragicomedia*'s sources? Did the two authors in fact have this volume before them? It was available, surely; the work was much copied during the Middle Ages and early Renaissance. It was printed twice in the 1490s, and although the

---

[26] The Elder Seneca, *Declamations,* ed. and trans. M. Winterbottom, 2 vols. (Cambridge, MA: Harvard Univ. Press; London: William Heinemann, 1974); the line from Marullus is on p. 488, from Cornelius Hispanus, p. 536, and from Argentarius, p. 554, all from Vol. II.

date is late, it is not impossible that Rojas might have seen it in this form. In any case, there is positive evidence that Seneca is indeed present in both parts of the *Celestina,* the first act and the rest. Castro Guisasola in his list of sources does not mention him, but María Rosa Lida de Malkiel does trace one *sententia* in the drama to his collection. Thus Castro Guisasola cites *Heroides* X, «Morsque minus poenae quam mora mortis habet» (l. 82). This, according to him, yields a line from the fifth act in the mouth of an impatient Calisto: «es mas penoso al delinquente esperar la cruda y capital sentencia, que el acto de la ya sabida muerte».[27] But as Lida de Malkiel points out, the last sentence in *Controversia,* III.5 would do equally well as a source: «crudelius est quam mori semper mortem timere».[28] She in fact pleads for both Ovid and Seneca on this point, as though Rojas had both texts before him. The case for the latter —stronger, to my mind— is that the expansion in the *Tragicomedia* reflects the content in the declamation: the speaker is being kept in suspense as to whether or not he is to die, and it is that situation which Calisto expresses in a figure. It is thus more than likely that Rojas knew Seneca. It is possible that the author of the first act also did. Thus, the *Controversia* Book III tells of a father arrested for disturbing the peace as he weeps on seeing his son die in a fire. The accused says at the beginning of his defense: «misero si flere no licet, magis flendum est» (I, 414). The line is a typical utterance for a declamation. It scores three times, as a general proposition or *sententia,* for the paradox, and for the etymological figure, *flere-flendum.* The last, as I think, may have inspired the sustained *adnominatio* in Act I of the *Tragicomedia* on «llorar».

> CELESTINA: Pármeno, ¿tú no vees que es necedad o simpleza llorar por lo que con llorar no se puede remediar?
> PÁRMENO: Por esso lloro, que si con llorar fuesse possible traer a mi amo el remedio, tan grande sería el plazer de la tal esperança, que de gozo no podría llorar. Pero assí, perdida ya toda la esperança, pierdo el alegría y lloro. (I.132)

We have the same figure and virtually the same word. The sense of the two fragments is not wholly dissimilar. Seneca's character says that one should weep because weeping is forbidden, Pármeno because weeping is useless. Our ground thus seems to be well covered. Unless we can propose other sources for our two fragments, we are fairly safe in saying that both authors at some time had Seneca's text in their hands.

The reason above all why it seems to me worthwhile to include Seneca as part of the background of *Celestina* is that declamation may help us to understand one of the most conspicuous features of the play, the

---

[27] CASTRO GUISASOLA, p. 69; the line from *Celestina* is the latter part of V.20.
[28] *Originalidad,* p. 341; the quotation from Seneca is in I.408.

long argumentative speech. Generally, the extended utterances of the characters are of several kinds: some are affective or introspective, some narrative, some descriptive. One of the most important structurally, however, is the speech intended to persuade. Lida de Malkiel very characteristically speaks of the didactic speech:

> con gran acopio de sentencias, como en las consideraciones de Sempronio y Calisto sobre la liberalidad, la honra, la tristeza y el consuelo, y en las de Pleberio y Alisa sobre la instabilidad de la vida, las ventajas de casar a la hija y su ignorancia original. (pp. 108-09).

Gilman refers to this species generally, and more accurately, saying that argument is one of the basic modes of discourse in *Celestina* (along with sentiment) (*The Art,* p. 25). For reasons that already may be obvious it seems plausible to me that the «sententiae», so called, recorded in Seneca may be the primary model for this last form of speech. I must emphasize that argument in the dialogue is a prominent feature of the *Tragicomedia* way beyond the ordinary demands of drama, or indeed of belles-lettres generally: the characters argue more here than they do in the plays of Terence and Plautus for example, more even than in the humanistic plays which meet *Celestina* half way. The elegant, «witty, conceited» bits of declamation recorded by Seneca are, of course, nothing but argument, and are, as we have seen, loaded down with the traits of style normally associated with Silver Latin. The coincidence is striking, and is surely not trivial: where else could the pattern in our play, argument-plus-figures come from?

I should stress that we are not dealing with impressions. As I have tried to show earlier in this study, the forms of argument exploited by the speakers in *Celestina* are such in a fully technical sense. Rational conviction can be produced in a listener mainly in two ways, by deduction from premises, or by induction from examples. Both procedures figure large in the utterances of Celestina, Sempronio and the rest. How else is one to characterize some of their mountainous speeches than as accumulations of examples, meant to prove a point? As for deduction the matter is even clearer. Commonplaces, *sententiae,* in the speeches are common indeed, as we know very well, and wherever there is a commonplace there is a virtual syllogism or enthymeme. In *Celestina* notably, the universal proposition serves as the major of a syllogism: the special case is assimilated to a general rule. The old woman recommends herself saying «Aquél es rico que está bien con Dios». By implication she is saying that she herself is at peace with God (minor), and that she is truly rich, against appearances (conclusion). Thus it is not enough to say that the *Tragicomedia* is sententious: if it is sententious, it is also argumentative. And beyond this, one could say that much of the logical apparatus of the orator is generally at the disposal of the speakers in the play.

The characters argue: they speak in *suasoriae*. More particularly, they argue with each other. As I have pointed out above, at times in *Celestina* there are series of persuasive speeches disposed sandwich-wise, alternately pro and con some proposal. In Act II Calisto asks Sempronio to see the old woman home, and advances reasons why he should. The servant, reluctant, offers arguments to the contrary. Each speaker then has a second go, and so we have a respectable debate, with two speeches pro, two contra. Celestina urges Elicia to learn to repair maidenheads and Elicia refuses. The two women argue like lawyers. Celestina and Pármeno dispute monumentally in Act I on a variety of subjects, mainly on the boy's continued fidelity to his master. Most important of all, Calisto and Sempronio near the beginning of the play argue at length very formally whether the former should love Melibea. The pro and con, the well-designed arguments on both sides, duplicate exactly the state of things in declamation. Should the Spartans retreat from Thermopylae? Should Cicero destroy his writings? Some speak in favor, some against.

What does a *suasoria* or a *controversia* actually look like? How is it disposed, at large or in detail? Again, one would have to remark that certain of them are very much like speeches in *Celestina*: they are sententious, full of antitheses, and repetitious. I quote, without prior comment, Seneca the Elder's selection from a *suasoria* by Albucius Silus, urging Alexander the Great not to cross the seas:

> Terrae quoque suum finem habent, et ipsius mundi aliquis occasus est; nihil infinitum est; modum tu magnitudini facere debes, quoniam Fortuna non facit. Magni pectoris est inter secunda moderatio. Eundem Fortuna victoriae tuae quem naturae finem facit: imperium tuum cludit Oceanus. O quantum magnitudo tua rerum quoque natural supergressa est! Alexander orbi magnus est, Alexandro orbis angustus est. Aliquis etiam magnitudini modus est; non procedit ultra spatia sua caelum, maria intra terminos suos agitantur. Quidquid ad summum pervenit, incremento non relinquit locum. Non magis quicquam ultra Alexandrum novimus quam ultra Oceanum. (II.488).

This speech, all on one subject, could just possibly be transplanted into *Celestina* without arousing suspicion. The series of examples, the *sententiae* —«nihil infinitum est», «magni pectoris», etc.—, the antitheses, paradoxes, even the exclamation that breaks up the series of declarative sentences is characteristic: this could be one of Celestina's quietly persuasive utterances. Even more remarkable in this sense is the long harangue by Fuscus the Elder urging the Spartans not to abandon Thermopylae; it begins:

> At, puto, rudis lecta aetas et animus qui frangeretur metu, insuetaque arma non passurae manus hebetataque senio aut vulneribus corpora. Quid dicam? potissimos Graeciae? an Lacedaemonios? an electos? An repetam tot acies patrum totque excidia urbium, tot victarum gentium spolia? et nunc pro-

duntur condita sine moenibus templa? Pudet consilii nostri, pudet, etiamsi non fugimus, deliberasse talia. (II.506, 508)

The sarcasm *(illusio)*, the anaphora, the series of rhetorical questions, indeed the variety itself, and the heavy load of affect recall some of the old bawd's speeches, Sempronio's grand piece on mutability, many others. Selections of this sort are very common in Seneca's collection, especially among the *suasoriae*: those of the «Asiatic» Fuscus are especially brilliant and emotional. The uninterrupted sequence of commonplaces on one theme, so characteristic of the *Tragicomedia,* can also be found among Seneca's examples. Publius Asprenas has: «Fortunae lex est praestare quae exegeris. Miserere: mutabilis est casus; dederunt victis terga victores et quos provexerat fortuna destituit» (I.30), Porcius Latro has: «fragilis et caduca felicitas est, et omnis blandientis fortunae speciosus cum periculo nitor: et sine causa saepe fovit et sine ratione destituit» (I.204). Fabianus offers us:

> Noli pecuniam concupiscere. Quid tibi dicam? Haec est quae auget discordiam urbis et terrarum orbem in bellum agitat, humanum genus cognatum natura in fraudes et scelera et mutuum odium instigat, haec est quae senes corrumpit. Quidam summum bonum dixerunt voluptatem et omnia ad corpus rettulerunt. (I.346)

Sometimes the string of *sententiae* is longer. Fuscus the Elder has a splendid parade of *loci* on death:

> si cadendum est, erratis si metuendam creditis mortem. Nulli natura in aeternum spiritum dedit, statque nascentibus in finem vitae dies. Ex inbecilla enim nos materia deus orsus est; quippe minimis succidunt corpora. Indenuntiata sorte rapimur; sub eodem pueritia fato est, eadem iuventus causa cadit. Optamus quoque plerumque mortem; adeo in securam quietem recessus ex vita est. At gloriae nullus finis est proximique deos sic ageses agunt; feminis quoque frequens hoc in mortem pro gloria iter est. (II.508, 510)

Seneca himself in the preface to Book I of the *Controversiae* has a fine piece on the corruption of his time:

> Torpent ecce ingenia desidiosae iuventutis nec in unius honestae rei labore vigilatur; somnus languorque ac somno et languore turpior malarum rerum industria invasit animos: cantandi saltandique obscena studia effeminatos tenent, et capillum frangere et ad muliebres blanditias extenuare vocem, mollitia corporis certare cum feminis et inmundissimis se excolere munditiis nostrorum adulescentium specimen est. Quis aequalium vestrorum quid dicam satis ingeniosus, satis studiosus, immo quis satis vir est? Emolliti enervesque quod nati sunt in vita manent, expugnatores alienae pudicitiae, neglegentes suae. (I.8)

Sometimes Seneca reports in the third person passages like these. We get Fabianus' argument:

> At rationem aliam primam fecit: modum inponendum esse rebus secundis. Hic dixit sententiam: illa demum est magna felicitas quae arbitrio suo

97

constitit. Dixit deinde locum de varietate fortunae et, cum descripsisset nihil esse stabile, omnia fluitare et incertis motibus modo attolli, modo deprimi, absorberi terras et maria siccari, montes subsidere... (II.496)

All of these passages are plainly the same sort of discourse as Sempronio's great speech on liberality, or as dozens of others. Also typical of *Celestina* is the *sententia* or group of *sententiae* followed by supporting examples. In at least one instance the latter are one of Rojas' additions of the early 1500s: his hand is visible as he shapes his text deliberately along these lines (Areúsa's speech, IX,45-46). Here is Triarius quoted by Seneca:

Non ex formula natura respondet nec ad praescriptum casus obsequitur; semper expectari fortuna mavult quam regi. Aliubi effunditur inprovisa segetum maturitas, aliubi sera magno fenore moram redemit. Licet lex dies finiat, natura non recipit. (I.326)

The strong alliance between argument and fine phrases, essential to declamation and prominent in *Celestina,* is to my mind distinctive. This tie-up is above all what might convince us that our two authors were influenced by Seneca's collections. Further evidence, less powerful, perhaps, is the palpable similarity, line by line, by look and feel of a *suasoria* or *controversia* to certain speeches in the *Tragicomedia.* Here obviously we are on less certain ground. If declamation influenced other literary species and shares with them certain traits of style, how can we tell whether our Spanish text inherited them from one or the other? Indeed, literary texts other than declamatory are present in *Celestina,* and it would be foolish to assert that those had no part in shaping its personality. In fact, the case for a direct Senecan influence is twofold. In the first place it is plausible. The collections of *controversiae* and *suasoriae* are textbooks. They indeed do not teach by precept, but they do by example. For a fifteenth-century student or man of letters they would be in a class with works like the *Margarita poetica* of Albrecht von Eyb, in Rojas' library at his death.[29] This is a complete rhetoric made up entirely of examples: under «exordium» we get not the rules for composing this part of a speech, but a string of model *exordia,* under *narratio,* ditto, and so on. It is in the order of things likely that a work of this sort exerts an influence precisely if it is meant to. The texts are put before the reader for no other reason than that they be imitated, and if students and others do imitate them, one is hardly surprised. One would in principle, other things being equal, expect that models of this sort would outscore others in influence, and if the text was prestigious enough, one could reasonably look for traces of it everywhere. It is thus not wholly senseless to think of Seneca's texts as shaping in distinctive ways the design of *Celestina.*

[29] STEPHEN GILMAN, *The Spain of Fernando de Rojas,* p. 324.

In the second place we might simply observe, look down our noses. It is a plain fact that there are not many Silver Age texts that resemble declamations as much as do some of the speeches in *Celestina*. The broader traits of style are of course shared by non-declamatory writings, but in a curious way the utterances of Pármeno, Sempronio and the rest are often closer to the declamatory mode than comparable bits by Lucan, Statius and their like. Thus, one of the prime candidates for presumed declamatory influence is the great debate over the arms of Achilles in Book XIII of the *Metamorphoses* (Bonner, p. 151). But it takes no fine critical eye to see that the speeches of Ulysses and Ajax are not much like the harangues in the *Tragicomedia*. Or to take a case I have already mentioned, the soliloquy of Narcissus which so aroused Dryden's ire. Repetitive, assuredly. But Ovid, supreme and exquisite poet, covers his tracks: the impression is not at all of something static, but on the contrary mobile and nervous, expressing the changing moods of the desperate boy. Ovid's art effectively hides the fact that he is crisscrossing the same bit of territory over dozens of lines. There is nothing in *Celestina* like this: repetition is there, undisguised, without apologies.

I conclude this study by raising one difficulty. The following is a typically sententious speech from the *Tragicomedia*:

> como Séneca dize, los peregrinos tienen muchas posadas y pocas amistades, porque en breve tiempo con ninguno no pueden firmar amistad. Y el que está en muchos cabos, no está en ninguno; ni puede aprovechar el manjar, a los cuerpos, que en comiendo se lança, ni ay cosa que más la sanidad impida, que la diversidad y mudança y varïación de los manjares. Y nunca la llaga viene a cicatrizar en la cual muchas melezinas se tientan, ni convalece la planta que muchas vezes es traspuesta. Y no ay cosa tan provechosa, que en llegando apriessa aproveche. (I.142-44)

The «Seneca» in this case is, of course, not the Elder, but the Younger, and the passage is a textual quotation from the second epistle to Lucilius (Castro Guisasola, p. 94). I may seem to be subverting my whole argument. Precisely the sort of speech that can most easily be connected to declamation turns out in this case to be an identifiable fragment by a non-declaimer. Hundreds of passages in the letters to Lucilius are of just this kind. And in fact, the writings of the philosopher Seneca might do nearly as well as those of his father as models for *Celestina*'s declamatory style.[30] Why prefer one to the other? Several observations could be made. The first is an obvious one: the younger Seneca's texts are declamatory. They are so both structurally, and in genesis. One would scarcely want to deny an influence of father on son. Anecdote aside, it is the case that philosophical and moral topics were for years classic subjects for declamatory debate —«is the world governed by Providence?» or «should a man

---

[30] While this book was in press, LOUISE FOTHERGILL-PAYNE's *Seneca and «Celestina»* was published by Cambridge University Press (1988).

marry?». There plainly must have been some prior disposition on the part of *Celestina*'s authors that would attract them to texts organized like those of the great Stoic sage. These served handily both as source and as models because their rhetorical characteristics were the ones Rojas and his predecessor thought elegant and appropriate. Then too, one could raise the question of why these texts of Seneca best known to Rojas and his contemporaries should become models for speeches in a drama. The answer is unclear, but it might be safe to say that the authors of *Celestina* were not the only ones to get the idea: in a sense Seneca himself might have set the example. But the same question asked about the speeches quoted in the Elder Seneca suggests a much more obvious answer: declamations are in many ways patently dramatic. They were addressed to someone, a fictitious judge, Agamemnon, Cicero, or the Athenians threatened by Xerxes. What is more, they are at least potentially part of a dialogue. The speaker who counsels Cicero not to compromise with Antony can expect to be answered by one who urges the opposite. As we have seen, there are bits of dialogue in *Celestina* which simulate very closely this sort of exchange. The style, then, of our great tragicomedy assuredly does not come from one source, but declamation comes perhaps as close as anything to providing the bones and sinews of some of its most characteristic parts.[31]

[31] I add as a final note some further difficulties that could challenge the argument I have presented here. The actual words of the Elder Seneca, for example, might give the impression that good declamation was hostile to the traits I have thought were common to *controversiae* and *suasoriae* and *Celestina*. Seneca is a man of Attic taste, and deplores the bombast and repetitiousness of certain declaimers. He cautions against excessive use of *loci/sententiae*. He leaves the impression that since declamation is mock debate, the argumentative side of some of the speeches is not very strong. On the first two issues I comment in two ways. First, the examples speak for themselves. Some, indeed many, of the ones which recall *Celestina* are repetitious and sententious. Second, in the light of Seneca's own examples and practice, his warnings about excesses can hardly be considered prohibitions. On the third issue I should remark simply that debates are debates. A speaker in a mock debate may be more admired for his fine phrases than for his convincing arguments, but in some guise or another he is trying to prove something. And once again, Seneca's examples tell us what we need to know: they do sound argumentative. Another potential challenge to my views is found in an article by T. F. HIGHAM, «Ovid and Rhetoric», in *Ovidiana*, ed. N. I. Herescu (Paris: Les Belles Lettres, 1958), pp. 32-48. In this paper Higham, on the basis of both Ovid's texts and Seneca's remarks about him, tries to dissociate Ovid from declamation. I shall not attempt to paraphrase his argument in detail or to pass judgment on what appears to be a declaration of nonconformity. Higham cites Seneca's remark that Ovid preferred *suasoriae* to *controversiae* because argument there counted for less. This for us counts as a case against the *suasoria* as argument. But once again, the proof of the pudding is in the eating: the pieces of *suasoriae* Seneca quotes look argumentative. Higham also argues that «theme and variations» is not an inheritance from declamation. Without pretending any professional knowledge here, I should observe that themes and variations, though not necessarily a monopoly of declamation, are prominent there, and become prominent in other literary genres shortly after the time it starts to become a craze.

LIST OF WORKS CITED

ANON.: *Ad Herennium.* Ed. and trans. H. Caplan. Cambridge, MA: Harvard University Press; London: William Heinemann, 1954.
— *«Veterator» und «Advocatus».* Ed. J. Bolte. Berlin: Max Herrmann, 1902.
— *La vida de Lazarillo de Tormes y de sus fortunas y adversidades,* ed. Alberto Blecua. Clásicos Castalia, 58. Madrid: Castalia, 1974.

BARTHES, ROLAND: «L'Effet du réel». *Communications,* 11 (1968), 84-89.
BATAILLON, MARCEL: «La *Célestine* primitive». In *Studia philologica et litteraria in honorem L. Spitzer,* pp. 39-55. Bern: Francke, 1958. (Appears as Ch. 2 of the following item.)
— *La «Célestine» selon Fernando de Rojas.* Paris: Didier, 1961.
— «Gaspar von Barth, interprète de *La Célestine».* *Revue de Littérature Comparée,* 31 (1957), 321-40. (Appears as an appendix in the preceding item.)
BONNER, S.: *Roman Declamation.* Liverpool: University Press, 1949.

CASTRO, AMÉRICO: *El pensamiento de Cervantes. Revista de Filología Española,* anejo 6. Madrid: Centro de Estudios Históricos, 1925.
CASTRO GUISASOLA, F.: *Observaciones sobre las fuentes literarias de «La Celestina».* *Revista de Filología Española,* anejo 5. Madrid: Centro de Estudios Históricos, 1924.
CICERO: *De inventione, De optimo genere oratorum, Topica.* Ed. and trans. H. M. Hubbell. Cambridge, MA: Harvard University Press; London: William Heinemann, 1949.

D'ALTON, J. F.: *Roman Literary Theory and Criticism.* New York: Russell and Russell, 1962.
DONATUS: *Commenti Donatiani.* 2 vols. Leiden: A. W. Sijthoff, 1901-02.
— *Aeli Donati commentium Terenti.* Ed. P. Wessner. 2 vols. Leipzig: Teubner, 1902-03.
DRYDEN, JOHN: *An Essay of Dramatic Poesy and Other Critical Writings.* Ed. John L. Mahoney. Indianapolis: Bobbs Merrill, 1965.
DUCKWORTH, GEORGE: *The Nature of Roman Comedy.* Princeton: Univ. Press, 1952.

FLUCHÈRE, HENRI: *Shakespeare and the Elizabethans.* New York: Hill and Wang, 1956.
FORSTER, E. M.: *Aspects of the Novel.* London: Edward Arnold; New York: Harcourt Brace, 1927.
FRAKER, C. F.: «María Rosa Lida de Malkiel on the *Celestina».* *Hispania,* 50 (1967), 174-81.
FRULOVISI: *Titi Livii de Frulovisiis de Ferraria opera hactenus inedita.* Ed. C. W. Previté-Orton. Cambridge: Univ. Press, 1932.

101

GEERTZ, CLIFFORD: *The Interpretation of Cultures*. New York: Basic Books, 1973.
GILMAN, STEPHEN: *The Art of «La Celestina»*. Madison: University of Wisconsin Press, 1956.
— *The Spain of Fernando de Rojas: The Intellectual and Social Landscape of «La Celestina»*. Princeton: Univ. Press, 1972.
GREEN, OTIS H.: «The Artistic Originality of the *Celestina*». *Hispanic Review*, 33 (1965), 15-31.

HERMOGENES: *De ideis*, in *Opera*. Ed. Hugo Rabe. Portions translated in *Ancient Literary Criticism*. Ed. D. A. Russell and M. Winterbottom. Oxford: Clarendon Press, 1972.
HERRICK, MARVIN T.: *Comic Theory in the Sixteenth Century*. Urbana: Univ. of Illinois Press, 1964.
HIGHAM, T. F.: «Ovid and Rhetoric». In *Ovidiana*. Ed. N. I. Herescu. Paris: Les Belles Lettres, 1958, pp. 32-48.
HUNTER, R. L.: *The New Comedy of Greece and Rome*. Cambridge: Univ. Press, 1985.

KENNEY, E. J.: «The Style of the *Metamorphoses*». In *Ovid*. Ed. J. W. Binns. London: Routledge & Kegan Paul, 1973, pp. 116-53.
KUHN, THOMAS: *The Structure of Scientific Revolutions*. Chicago: Chicago Univ. Press, 1970.

LIDA DE MALKIEL, MARÍA ROSA: *La originalidad artística de «La Celestina»*. Buenos Aires: Eudeba, 1962.
LINDBERG, GERTRUD: *Studies in Hermogenes and Eustathios*. Lund: J. Lindell, 1977.
LOWES, JOHN LIVINGSTON: «The Loveres Maladye of *Hereos*». *Modern Philology*, 11 (1913-14), 1-56.

MANITIUS, MAX: *Handschriften antiker Autoren in mittelalterlichen Bibliotekskatalogen*. Leipzig: Otto Harrassowitz, 1935.
MENÉNDEZ Y PELAYO, MARCELINO: *Orígenes de la novela*. Buenos Aires: GLEM, 1944.

NEBRIJA, ANTONIO DE: *Artis rhetoricae cõpendiosa coaptatio ex Aristotile, Cicerone et Quintiliano*. Compluti: Arnaldo Guillermo de Brocar, 1515.

PANDOLFI, VITO, and ARTESE, ERMINIA (ed.): *Teatro goliardico dell'Umanesimo*, Milano: Lerici, 1965.
PEACHAM, HENRY: *The Garden of Eloquence* [facsimile of the 1593 edition with portions of the 1577]. Ed. W. G. Crane. Gainesville FL: Ecolar's Facsimiles and Reprints, 1954.

QUINTILIAN: *The «Institutio Oratoria»*. Ed. and trans. H. E. Butler. 4 vols. Cambridge, MA: Harvard Univ. Press; London: William Heinemann, 1920-22.

ROBBINS, EDWIN, W.: *Dramatic Characterization in Printed Commentaries on Terence 1473-1600*. Urbana: Univ. of Illinois Press, 1951.
ROJAS, FERNANDO DE: *La Celestina*. Ed. Julio Cejador y Frauca. 2 vols. Clásicos Castellanos, 20 and 28. Madrid: La Lectura, 1913; rpt. Espasa-Calpe, 1958.
— *Celestina: Tragicomedia de Calisto y Melibea*. Ed. Miguel Marciales. 2 vols. Illinois Medieval Monographs, 1. Urbana: Univ. of Illinois Press, 1985.
RYLE, GILBERT: *The Concept of Mind*. New York: Barnes and Noble, 1949.

SAMONÀ, CARMELO: *Aspetti del retoricismo nella «Celestina»*. Roma: Studi di Letteratura Spagnola, 2. Facoltà di Magisterio dell'Università di Roma, 1953.
SENECA, THE ELDER: *Declamations*. Ed. and trans. M. Winterbottom. 2 vols. Cambridge, MA: Harvard Univ. Press; London: William Heinemann, 1974.
SPITZER, LEO: «A New Book on the *Celestina*». *Hispanic Review*, 25 (1957), 1-25.
STUBBS, G. EDWARD: *The Church Service Book*. London: Novello, 1906.

TERENCE: *P. Terenti Afri Comoediae*. Ed. Robert Kauer and Wallace K. Lindsay. Oxford: Clarendon Press, 1958.
— *The Comedies*. Trans. Betty Radice. Harmondsworth: Penguin Books, 1965.

URREA, PEDRO MANUEL [XIMÉNEZ] DE: *Penitencia de amor*. Ed. R. Foulché-Delbosc. Biblioteca Hispánica, 10. Barcelona: L'Avenç, 1902.

VALLATA, JOHANNES DE: *Poliodorus: comedia humanística desconocida*. Ed. José María Casas Homs. Madrid: CSIC, 1953.

WHEATLEY, KATHERINE ERNESTINE: *Molière and Terence: A Study in Molière's Realism*. Univ. of Texas Bulletin, 3130. Austin: Univ. of Texas Press, 1931.
WILLIAMS, GORDON: *Change and Decline*. Berkeley: California Univ. Press, 1978.

BIBLIOGRAPHY